Second Edition

PROJECT BASED LEARNING HANDBOOK

A Guide to

Standards-Focused

Project Based Learning

for Middle and

High School Teachers

BUCK INSTITUTE FOR EDUCATION

About the Buck Institute for Education

The Buck Institute for Education (BIE) is a research and development organization working to make schools and classrooms more effective through the use of problem and project based instruction. Founded in 1987, BIE receives permanent funding from the Leonard and Beryl Buck Trust, and funding for specific projects from foundations, schools and school districts, state educational agencies, and the federal government.

PRINCIPAL AUTHOR
Thom Markham
SECONDARY AUTHORS
John Larmer
Jason Ravitz, PhD

BIE would like to thank John Thomas and the secondary authors of the first edition of this handbook, John R. Mergendoller and Andrew Michaelson. Their work provided a strong foundation for the present volume.

ISBN 0-9740343-0-4

Designed and produced by Wilsted & Taylor Publishing Services, Oakland, California.
COPYEDITING
Caroline Roberts
DESIGN AND COMPOSITION
Melissa Ehn
PRODUCTION MANAGEMENT
Christine Taylor

Printed and bound in Hong Kong through QuinnEssentials Books and Printing, Inc.

Contents

Great projects begin with planning for the end result. In this section, you'll learn to conceive manageable projects with engaging themes and high standards.

Manage the Process   **97**

As a PBL teacher, you can successfully manage the process of learning by using tools and strategies that bring structure and accountability to the process. This section offers specific recommendations for managing and evaluating a project.

IMPLEMENTING PROJECTS

Project Examples   **127**

What Do PBL Teachers Say?   **151**

Project Planning Form   **179**

Acknowledgments

In 1999, John Thomas (with the help of Andrew Michaelson and myself) prepared the first edition of the Buck Institute for Education Project Based Learning Handbook. Since then, thousands of educators throughout the United States and in other countries have used the Handbook, and it has played an important part in the spread of project based teaching strategies.

This second edition of the Project Based Learning Handbook incorporates the collective wisdom of the many teachers who piloted draft versions of the Handbook, as well as those who subjected it to rigorous critique. The educators who have purchased the Handbook or attended our Project Based Learning (PBL) Training Workshops have also provided new insights and inspiration. Although it is impossible to acknowledge the contributions of each individual, we are deeply grateful to all of them for the time they have given to improve the Handbook and the quality of their suggestions.

Like most practice-based work, some of the Handbook's ideas and documents are based upon the work of others. Where possible, we acknowledge sources. We are especially grateful to Bob Lenz, Thom Markham, Elizabeth Brown, and Ron Berger. Their projects provide outstanding examples of what PBL can become. John Thomas's theorizing about PBL and his research and analysis of successful project implementation remain at the core of this revised edition. We benefited greatly from the observations of Linda Ullah, Bo De Long-Cotty, Peter Iacono, Paul Curtis, and Jim Cleere, and their suggestions definitely improved the final product. Finally, examples from PBL teachers Kathleen O'Brien, Megan Pacheco, and Mark McKay were very helpful.

Although the Handbook synthesizes the thinking, experience, and insight of many individuals, Thom Markham is the person who wrote the bulk of the second edition. His own experience as a project based teacher, his knowledge of school reform, and his commitment to academic excellence have been invaluable. Similarly, John Larmer's understanding of standards-focused teaching and his assistance with the assessment sections of the Handbook have been a major contribution.

We hope this second edition of the Project Based Learning Handbook will provide the support needed for secondary teachers to venture into and succeed within the world of Project Based Learning.

John R. Mergendoller, PhD
EXECUTIVE DIRECTOR
BUCK INSTITUTE FOR EDUCATION

About the Handbook

There are many models of Project Based Learning. This Handbook reflects a specific model developed by the Buck Institute for Education (BIE). This model draws on the experiences of teachers who successfully use PBL in their classrooms, as well as recent research on student learning. It also incorporates the best practices of educators and organizations around the country who disseminate information on PBL.

The purpose of the Handbook is to guide teachers through all phases of successful PBL, from deciding on a project theme to reflecting on the outcomes of a project. The Handbook is designed to support both experienced and novice PBL teachers. It can be used as a supplement to the BIE Training Workshops in PBL, which are conducted regularly throughout the year, or as a stand-alone guide to PBL. Regardless of how you use it, we believe the Handbook will enable you to design high-quality projects in your classroom.

STANDARDS-FOCUSED PROJECT BASED LEARNING

Since the first edition of this Handbook in 1999, over 5,000 teachers have successfully used the BIE model to implement projects in schools across the United States and abroad. The new edition retains the tools and ideas that teachers have found useful but introduces a more refined guide to planning projects. Most important, the new Handbook takes special note of the need to design *standards-focused* projects that reflect today's emphasis on content, accountability, and performance.

We believe that the learning of specified subject-matter concepts and standards should be at the heart of PBL. Our projects begin with curriculum standards and use aligned assessments to determine what students have learned. They are designed around a Driving Question that knits together intended outcomes and project activities. Finally, they incorporate vital workplace skills and lifelong habits of learning, and they help teachers draw on the resources of the community to move project boundaries beyond the four walls of the classroom.

IMPORTANT NOTES
ABOUT THE BIE MODEL OF
PROJECT BASED LEARNING

BIE's goal is to establish standards-focused PBL as a central strategy by which specific curricular goals and standards can be attained. In other words, we have not written this Handbook to help teachers "do projects." Projects are too often the students' reward for learning in traditional ways—they are the "icing" rather than the "cake." For example, after lecturing about the parts of the Constitution in a government or social studies class and assigning textbook reading for homework, a teacher might break students into groups and ask them to write a constitution for a new lunar settlement. In this case, the project follows the learning as dessert follows the main course. This lunar constitution assignment could be an interesting and challenging project, but it does not fall within our understanding of PBL. For us, PBL is the central framework upon which the teaching and learning of core concepts is built, not a supplementary enrichment activity to be undertaken after the hard work of learning is done.

At the same time, another important message in this Handbook is that PBL should not replace all other methods in the classroom. The BIE model encourages teachers to rely on their experience and expertise to blend projects and conventional methods of instruction into an integrated whole that provides students with a rich blend of content, skills, and opportunities for academic and personal growth.

PROJECT BASED LEARNING
VERSUS PROBLEM BASED LEARNING

In this Handbook, the term PBL refers to Project Based Learning. However, others use the term PBL when referring to Problem Based Learning. What is the difference between Project Based Learning and Problem Based Learning? First, few people agree on the precise meaning of these terms, and they are often used interchangeably. Both describe a process of using "ill-structured" problems that are deliberately designed to require students to learn content-specific knowledge and problem-solving skills as they seek diverse solutions to meaningful questions.

In the BIE vocabulary, Project Based Learning is a general term describing an instructional method that uses projects as the central focus of instruction in a variety of disciplines. Often, projects emerge out of an authentic context, address controversial or significant issues in the community, and unfold in unexpected ways. In contrast, BIE's design for Problem Based Learning uses realistic scenarios and role-plays to lead students along a more carefully planned path toward a set of prescribed outcomes.* Regardless of how it is labeled, a project must be rooted in content standards and allow for student-centered inquiry into a meaningful question.

The Handbook is written for Project Based Learning, but it also introduces the terminology commonly used in the BIE Problem Based Economics (PBE) and Problem Based Government (PBG) units developed for high school teachers. For more information about these products, consult the BIE Website, *www.bie.org.*

USING THE HANDBOOK

This Handbook presents a systematic guide to the design and implementation of standards-focused projects and is divided into the following sections:

- An **Introduction** to Project Based Learning that presents the case for PBL and outlines the core objectives of PBL.
- A description of the **Design and Planning** process for creating successful standards-focused projects, along with **Idea Banks** of project resources and useful forms.
- **Examples** of typical projects.
- A section entitled **What Do PBL Teachers Say?**, offering expert advice and management tips from teachers who have successfully implemented projects in their classrooms.
- A **Project Planning Form** that can be used to plan your own project. This form can be copied from the Handbook and is available on the BIE Website.

*See N. Maxwell, Y. Bellisimo, and J. R. Mergendoller, "Problem Based Learning: Modifying the Medical Model for Teaching High School Economics," *The Social Studies* 92, no. 2: 75–78.

USING THE BIE WEBSITE

For additional PBL resources, including examples of projects, links to PBL organizations, and forms and materials for PBL, go to *www.bie.org.* The BIE Website is designed to support the material in the PBL Handbook and assist teachers in locating resources for project planning, assessment, use of technology, and professional development. Additional copies of the Handbook also can be ordered from the Buck Institute for Education at 415-883-0122 or *www.bie.org.*

INTRODUCTION TO PROJECT BASED LEARNING

BEGIN WITH THE END IN MIND

CRAFT THE DRIVING QUESTION

PLAN THE ASSESSMENT

MAP THE PROJECT

MANAGE THE PROCESS

Contents

INTRODUCTION TO PROJECT BASED LEARNING

The introduction is designed to orient you to the field of Project Based Learning. Included in this section are a brief history of PBL and a description of its benefits. By the end of this section, you will be able to describe PBL and identify key elements of successful projects.

A BRIEF HISTORY OF PBL

For over 100 years, educators such as John Dewey have reported on the benefits of experiential, hands-on, student-directed learning. Most teachers, knowing the value of engaging, challenging projects for students, have planned field trips, laboratory investigations, and interdisciplinary activities that enrich and extend the curriculum. "Doing projects" is a long-standing tradition in American education.

The roots of PBL lie in this tradition. But the emergence of a method of teaching and learning called Project Based Learning is the result of two important developments over the last 25 years. First, there has been a revolution in learning theory. Research in neuroscience and psychology has extended cognitive and behavioral models of learning—which support traditional direct instruction—to show that knowledge, thinking, doing, and the contexts for learning are inextricably tied. We now know that learning is partly a social activity; it takes place within the context of culture, community, and past experiences. This is apparent in research on problem-based learning in the medical field, an important forerunner of PBL.

Research shows that learners not only respond by feeding back information, but they also actively use what they know to explore, negotiate, interpret, and create. They *construct* solutions, thus shifting the emphasis toward the process of learning. In addition, cognitive research has revealed much more about the nature of problem solving. Education has benefited from this research, as teachers have learned how to effectively scaffold content and activities to amplify and extend the skills and capabilities of students.

Second, the world has changed. Nearly all teachers understand how the industrial culture has shaped the organization and methods of schools in the 19th and 20th centuries, and they recognize that schools must now adapt to a new century. It is clear that children need both knowledge *and* skills to succeed. This need is driven not only by workforce demands for high-performance employees who can plan,

INTRODUCTION TO PROJECT BASED LEARNING

collaborate, and communicate, but also by the need to help all young people learn civic responsibility and master their new roles as global citizens.

In a sense, the need for education to adapt to a changing world is the primary reason that PBL is increasingly popular. PBL is an attempt to create new instructional practices that reflect the environment in which children now live and learn. And, as the world continues to change, so does our definition of PBL. The most important recent shift in education has been the increased emphasis on standards, clear outcomes, and accountability. Thus, one purpose of this edition of the BIE Project Based Learning Handbook is to incorporate the latest thinking on standards and assessment—to outline a planning process for *standards-focused* projects. But this process will continue to evolve. Remember that PBL is a field that you, as a practitioner, will help create by your actions and leadership in the classroom.

DEFINING STANDARDS-FOCUSED PBL

There is no one accepted definition of PBL. However, BIE defines standards-focused PBL as *a systematic teaching method that engages students in learning knowledge and skills through an extended inquiry process structured around complex, authentic questions and carefully designed products and tasks.* This definition encompasses a spectrum ranging from brief projects of one to two weeks based on a single subject in one classroom to yearlong, interdisciplinary projects that involve community participation and adults outside the school.

More important than the definition itself are the attributes of effective projects. You will find that the BIE planning model is based on a number of criteria that distinguish carefully planned projects from other extended activities in the classroom. Outstanding projects:

- Recognize students' inherent *drive to learn,* their capability to do important work, and their need to be taken seriously by putting them at the center of the learning process.
- Engage students in the central concepts and principles of a discipline. The project work is *central* rather than peripheral to the curriculum.
- Highlight provocative issues or questions that lead students to *in-depth exploration of authentic and important topics.*

- Require the use of essential *tools and skills,* including technology, for learning, self-management, and project management.
- Specify *products* that solve problems, explain dilemmas, or present information generated through investigation, research, or reasoning.
- Include *multiple products* that permit frequent feedback and consistent opportunities for students to learn from experience.
- Use *performance-based assessments* that communicate high expectations, present rigorous challenges, and require a range of skills and knowledge.
- Encourage *collaboration* in some form, either through small groups, student-led presentations, or whole-class evaluations of project results.

In standards-based PBL, students are pulled through the curriculum by a Driving Question or authentic problem that creates a need to know the material.

The BIE model for PBL also addresses a singular need in the field of PBL: to create *standards-focused* projects that fit well with the era of accountability and performance. Often, projects have been used as fun or change-of-pace events completed after students have been pushed through homework assignments, lectures, and tests. In standards-based PBL, students are pulled through the curriculum by a Driving Question or authentic problem that creates a need to know the material. The Driving Question is tied to content standards in the curriculum, and assessment is explicitly designed to evaluate the students' knowledge of the content.

Similarly, Project Based Learning is sometimes equated with inquiry-based or experiential learning. Though PBL shares some overlapping characteristics with these two terms, standards-focused PBL is designed to acknowledge the importance of standards and evaluation of student learning. In an era of accountability, with testing and performance uppermost in the minds of parents and educators, it is imperative that all instructional methods incorporate high standards, rigorous challenges, and valid assessment methods.

THE BENEFITS OF PBL

As a field, PBL is still in the developmental stage. For example, there is not sufficient research or empirical data to state that PBL is a proven alternative to other forms of instruction. Based on evidence gathered over the past ten years, PBL appears to be an equivalent or slightly better model for producing gains in academic achievement, although results vary with the quality of the project and the level of student engagement. Also, PBL is not appropriate as a method for teaching certain basic skills such as reading or computation; however, it does provide an environment for the application of those skills.

More important, evidence shows that PBL enhances the quality of learning and leads to higher-level cognitive development through students' engagement with complex, novel problems. It is also clear that PBL teaches students complex processes and procedures such as planning and communicating. Accomplishing these goals, however, requires time for both teachers and students to master the behaviors and strategies necessary for successful PBL.

PBL can help you as a teacher create a high-performing classroom in which you and your students form a powerful learning community focused on achievement, self-mastery, and contribution to the community.

In addition to research, convincing reports have come from teachers that PBL is a rigorous, relevant, and engaging instructional model that supports authentic inquiry and autonomous learning for students. Along with encouraging academic proficiency and meeting the traditional goals of education, PBL has important benefits for today's students. Teachers report that PBL:

- Overcomes the dichotomy between knowledge and thinking, helping students to both "know" and "do."
- Supports students in learning and practicing skills in problem solving, communication, and self-management.
- Encourages the development of habits of mind associated with lifelong learning, civic responsibility, and personal or career success.
- Integrates curriculum areas, thematic instruction, and community issues.
- Assesses performance on content and skills using criteria similar to those in the work world, thus encouraging accountability, goal setting, and improved performance.
- Creates positive communication and collaborative relationships among diverse groups of students.
- Meets the needs of learners with varying skill levels and learning styles.
- Engages and motivates bored or indifferent students.

As with any teaching method, PBL can be used effectively or ineffectively. At its best, PBL can help you as a teacher create a high-performing classroom in which you and your students form a powerful learning community focused on achievement, self-mastery, and contribution to the community. It allows you to focus on central ideas and salient issues in your curriculum, create engaging and challenging activities in the classroom, and support self-directed learning among your students.

PBL IN YOUR CLASSROOM

Planning for a project must take into account what is possible in your classroom. The scope of a project will be affected by the bell schedule, the time of year, standardized testing, and the other myriad factors that impact your work. Perhaps the first question that usually arises is: do I have time to do this project? To answer that question, it is helpful *not* to think of PBL as taking time away from the regular curriculum. Instead, consider a standards-focused project as a central method of teaching and learning that replaces conventional instruction for a portion of your course. Standards-focused projects teach students the same essential information you might teach them through lecture and discussion. PBL teachers also find that they do considerably less "busy work" activities in the classroom. And, though projects take time to plan, teachers have more time to work with students once a project is under way.

COVERAGE VERSUS "UNCOVERAGE"

It is true that projects do not lend themselves to covering a laundry list of topics, as too often happens in the classroom. But in the case of good education, less is more. If you are pressed for time and need to include many topics in your instruction during a year, you may want to think about the concept of "uncoverage." This means making a deliberate decision about topics that you want to teach in depth versus topics that can be simply "covered." What parts of your curriculum can be easily and successfully handled through lectures or textbook assignments? What parts require more depth? Identify those topics that reflect the most important ideas and concepts in your curriculum—and incorporate those topics into projects. Those are the topics with which you want students to grapple. The remaining topics you can deal with through direct instruction.

ARE YOUR STUDENTS CAPABLE?

Two questions regarding students immediately arise when you are thinking about a project. How much will they be involved? And, are they capable of a project, both behaviorally and academically? Student autonomy is one of the hallmarks of PBL. Still, most teachers introduce student autonomy in stages, depending upon students' age and experience. Before planning your project, think about how much you want your students to be involved in its design and how much autonomy they will have in carrying out project activities. You may want to select the project topic, particularly for the first project in your classroom. With students who are eager and prepared, you may wish to have them select the project topic and define the learning outcomes. Your role becomes one of coach and facilitator, helping students shape the project so that it meets content standards and allows for a variety of assessments.

Are your students ready and capable? That question can be answered based only on your experience and knowledge. The Handbook will offer you ideas on how to scaffold lessons for students in a way that prepares them for the academic knowledge, as well as for the skills, that may be required for them to succeed in the project. Often, teachers do not introduce projects until the midfall or later, giving them time to assess students and prepare them for project work. If students have not had experience with projects, it's worth remembering that they will need training in such skills as collaboration, research, project management, and oral presentations. Plus, you may have to manage them closely until they have mastered self-management skills.

YOUR STYLE AND SKILLS

Once teachers feel comfortable with PBL, they usually find teaching with projects to be more fulfilling and enjoyable. PBL is a way of working with students as they discover more about themselves and the world, and that brings job satisfaction. However, in addition to strong instructional and organizational skills, PBL requires that teachers facilitate and manage the *process* of learning. Rather than rely on the model of the child as an empty vessel to be filled, PBL teachers must create tasks and conditions under which student thinking can be revealed—a cocreative process that involves inquiry, dialogue, and skill building as the project proceeds.

Though most teachers recognize that active learning is vital, not all of us react in the same way to an open-ended process. Projects are sometimes described as chaotic or messy (though in a well-structured project, it only appears to be disorderly—it's really just the ambiguous problem-solving process that is under way). Prior to a project is a good time to reflect on your teaching style and skills. How will you operate in a PBL environment? Are you comfortable with children moving around a classroom or with the ambiguity that characterizes a more open-ended learning process?

It may help to ask yourself this question: do you prefer to be a leader or a manager? Leaders facilitate problem solving in a group and help the group find their own solutions. Managers control the process and look for prescribed outcomes. In reality, good teachers go back and forth between the two roles. But if you are hesitant to release control over your students, you may want to avoid projects or start small until you feel comfortable and skilled in project leadership.

Once teachers feel comfortable with PBL, they usually find teaching with projects to be more fulfilling and enjoyable. PBL is a way of working with students as they discover more about themselves and the world, and that brings job satisfaction.

As a leader, your job is to help each student produce a superior product by facilitating learning. As students gather data and progress in their problem solving, they will encounter obstacles and opportunities. At the heart of successful PBL is your ability to support and direct students (or conversely, your ability to let them struggle with a problem or information as they search out answers and solutions). This requires interpersonal and communication skills, as well as the ability to define the agenda for the class and push a project through to a successful conclusion. It also includes being sensitive to the fact that students finish work at different rates, with different abilities, aptitudes, and learning styles.

PBL AND YOUR SCHOOL

PBL works extremely well in schools that have extended blocks of time instead of 50-minute periods. Similarly, when schools are formed around small learning communities such as academies or houses, PBL is a natural tool for teaching and learning. But if your school does not have these reforms in place, it is still possible to create excellent projects for students.

You will also find that good projects in classrooms encourage changes in the culture and structure of schools. Schools are under increasing pressure to raise standards, improve climate, and personalize education. PBL can contribute significantly to this process by encouraging teacher collaboration, motivating students to achieve, using the tools and language of project management and organizational change, and helping to incorporate school-wide learning outcomes into the curriculum. In particular, PBL fits well with efforts to create a high-performance school culture that values both rigor and relevance. In addition, projects are a great way to involve parents and community members in the educational process, a result that often leads to more support for the school and a better understanding of the needs of students.

A question often asked by teachers in low-performing schools is: can Project Based Learning work in my school? It can. For students with basic skills issues, it may be necessary to include more direct instruction during a project, design shorter projects, or tie projects closely to fewer and more specific standards. But PBL offers all students the opportunity to investigate authentic topics of interest to them, thus engaging them in the learning process in ways that traditional instruction does not.

BEGIN WITH THE END IN MIND

CRAFT THE
DRIVING
QUESTION

PLAN THE
ASSESSMENT

Designing
and
Planning
Successful
Projects

MAP THE
PROJECT

MANAGE
THE
PROCESS

Contents

BEGIN WITH THE END IN MIND

*Great projects begin with planning for the end result.
In this section, you'll learn to conceive manageable
projects with engaging themes and high standards.*

As you begin planning for your project, it is essential to gain a conceptual feel for the terrain and the journey ahead. Project Based Learning is a powerful, but challenging, instructional method that requires vision, structure, and a solid understanding of the learning process. Good projects do not occur by accident. They result from rigorous up-front planning that includes thoughtful outcomes, timelines, and management strategies.

By beginning with the end in mind, you will improve your ability to plan projects, as well as communicate the purpose and context of a project to your students. Students who understand the meaning of what they are learning retain more information, apply their knowledge more skillfully, and feel more motivated to achieve.

FIRST STEPS

In this part of the Handbook, you will find six steps that will help you to begin planning an effective project:

- Develop a project idea
- Decide the scope of the project
- Select standards
- Incorporate simultaneous outcomes
- Work from project design criteria
- Create the optimal learning environment

1 Develop a Project Idea

If an idea for a project doesn't strike you while you're walking down the hallway to your classroom or over lunch in the staff room, where do you get ideas for projects? Here are seven suggestions for developing project ideas and themes:

- **Work backward from a topic.** Project ideas come from articles, issues, current events, conversations, and wonderment. Often, they emerge from discussions between members of a teacher team. Once an idea comes to you, work backwards to shape the idea to meet your curriculum outcomes and standards.

- **Use your standards.** Standards represent a comprehensive summary of what is important in a discipline. As such, they often capture important themes that can form the basis for projects. Benchmarks for standards are also important indicators that can inspire and guide the design of products and assessments for projects. If they are available, you can also look at past statewide exams for ideas.

- **Find projects and ideas on the Web.** Many Websites offer project ideas and descriptions of successful projects in every discipline and at every grade level. For links, check the BIE Website, *www.bie.org*.

- **Map your community.** Outside the door of the classroom lies a multitude of projects. Using student groups to examine your local community can be an exciting, informative way to begin asking questions—and developing project themes. In the **Idea Bank** in this section, the community mapping process is described.

- **Match what people do in their daily work.** Projects can be modeled on questions and problems people face in their work life, the technical operations defining their craft, the workplace expectations shaping their day-to-day life, and problems that students encounter in their school lives.

- **Tie the project to local and national events.** Use projects to focus student attention on controversies and questions of the day.

- **Focus on community service.** Authentic projects can be developed easily around community needs. Look for nonprofit organizations that need help or expertise.

2 Decide the Scope of the Project

Projects range from shorter, more contained projects of one to two weeks to open-ended explorations lasting much longer. Often projects involve field research, interviews, library visits, and community inquiry. Decisions on the scope of activities in the project should be made before the project begins and should be based on students' experience and readiness, the school schedule, the subject, and your level of comfort and expertise.

Community-based projects that help students work with adults and investigate issues outside of the classroom are ideal, since PBL works well with authentic issues. Such open-ended investigations invite many different possible solutions to problems. If it is not possible

PROJECT SCOPE

	Small Project ◄────────► Ambitious Project	
Duration	Five to ten days	Most of the semester
Breadth	One topic One standard	Multiple disciplines Multiple standards
Technology	Limited	Extensive
Outreach	Classroom-based	Community-based
Partnership	One teacher	Multiple teachers and community members
Audience	Classroom or school	Expert panel

to have students leave the classroom for a project, consider bringing in adults from the community as guest artists or experts—not just for a day, but to work with students during the project.

The Audience for the Project

A vital consideration that shapes the scope of a project is the audience for the products that students will produce. An audience of community members or expert adults for a final presentation raises the stakes for students and elicits the best performances. Similarly, an audience composed only of members of the class generally will not evoke the same effort or produce the same results. But a project with an authentic audience may also require more time for students to master the project outcomes and prepare for a successful culminating presentation.

Student Autonomy

Students' experiences and capabilities also influence the scope of the project. Student autonomy is one of the hallmarks of PBL. Still, most teachers introduce student autonomy in stages, depending upon students' age and experience. Before planning your project, think about how much you want your students to be involved in its design.

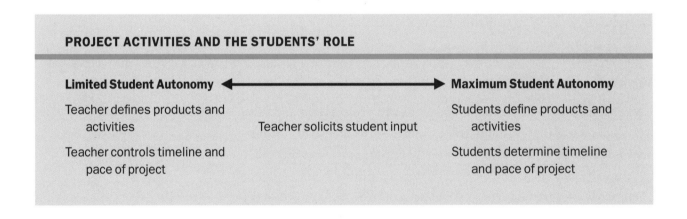

PROJECT DESIGN AND THE STUDENTS' ROLE

Limited Student Input		Maximum Student Input
Teacher selects topic	Teacher solicits student input	Students select topic
Teacher defines learning outcomes	Teacher and students negotiate learning outcomes	Students define learning outcomes

Similarly, projects vary in the autonomy students are given to define day-to-day project activities. Some teachers plan and schedule products and activities and expect students to accomplish things as planned. Other teachers allow students to suggest new products and take a more active role in defining the way the project will unfold.

PROJECT ACTIVITIES AND THE STUDENTS' ROLE

Limited Student Autonomy		Maximum Student Autonomy
Teacher defines products and activities	Teacher solicits student input	Students define products and activities
Teacher controls timeline and pace of project		Students determine timeline and pace of project

3 Select Standards

Accountability requires clear standards and solid assessment practices. In PBL—as in all good standards-based practices—the key question is: what do you want your students to know and be able to do? More informally, you might phrase the question this way: what topics would you be embarrassed about if your students couldn't discuss them intelligently at the end of the project?

The process of identifying standards begins before the project, often even before the start of the school year. Look over the state standards that guide your teaching and identify the key standards that you believe might be best met through project-based instruction.

One important tip is not to try to meet too many standards in a short project—no more than three standards per subject is best (if your project is interdisciplinary or longer-term, adjust accordingly). Including a laundry list of standards in the project design gives the illusion of meeting many educational goals, but assessing too many standards is difficult. You don't want to plan for any outcomes that you can't assess. If you have other standards that you hope the students will meet, that's fine. But they should not be the focus of your current project.

Projects often begin with a vision or idea sparked by a discussion or an article. If a project idea starts to develop in your mind, work backwards from the project idea and products to the standards you need to teach. The important task is to be clear about which standards will be assessed in the project and how the products will give all students the opportunity to demonstrate what they have learned.

A second source of standards and outcomes is your district or school-wide outcomes. Many districts and schools have gone through an extensive process of standards development and have adopted a set of outcomes based on community and teacher input. Incorporating one or two of these outcomes into the project helps make district or school-wide outcomes a reality.

Literacy as a Core Standard

The literacy of students is a central concern in schools. Including at least one literacy outcome in your project—along with a major product that can be used to assess writing, speaking, or reading strategies—is recommended for projects.

4 Incorporate Simultaneous Outcomes

PBL is not only a way of learning, it's also a way of working together to gather and present information. Collaboration is integral to successful projects; so are performance-based products such as exhibitions and oral presentations. A powerful aspect of PBL is that it allows teachers to simultaneously incorporate more than academic outcomes into classroom activities—in the form of specific skills and habits of mind—and to build students' capacity for skillful work.

Skills

The **Idea Bank** in this section of the Handbook will give you examples of skills that can be taught and assessed in projects. For example, the SCANS skills represent a list of workforce skills developed by a joint committee of the United States Departments of Labor and Education, based on extensive interviews with representatives of business and industry. This list and others focus attention on the need for students to be able to work in groups, manage projects, meet deadlines, present information, think critically, solve problems, and use technology wisely.

Habits of mind are the deeper qualities of learning and thinking that are vital to lifelong learning, success in the work world, and personal satisfaction.

As you begin your project design, identify one or two skills that students will use in the project. Think about how you will build in assessments for these skills. Note that skills are best assessed using performance-based measures aligned with a scoring guide such as a rubric. In the section of the Handbook on **Plan the Assessment**, we'll describe how to create and use a rubric.

Habits of Mind

Another category of outcomes is also possible: habits of mind. These are the deeper qualities of learning and thinking that are vital to lifelong learning, success in the work world, and personal satisfaction. The **Idea Bank** cites examples of habits of mind such as curiosity, flexibility, and perseverance, but feel free to choose your own. What qualities do you think are important for young people to nurture and develop? Choose one and incorporate it as an outcome for the project. Measuring such an outcome is challenging, as are any important intangibles in life. Use journals or individual debriefings with students to collect qualitative assessment information on habits of mind.

5 Work from Project Design Criteria

From the above considerations, it is clear that good projects don't just happen, but are based on important criteria that help you carefully structure the project and support its success. A simple set of criteria is listed in the Six A's in the **Idea Bank** in this section. Using these criteria, a project should include Authenticity, Academic Rigor, Applied Learning, Active Exploration, Adult Connections, and thoughtful Assessment Practices.

As you plan your project, ask yourself if the project meets other important criteria. Does the project:

- Meet standards?
- Engage students?
- Focus on essential understanding?
- Encourage higher-level thinking?
- Teach literacy and reinforce basic skills?
- Allow all students to succeed?
- Use clear, precise assessments?
- Require the sensible use of technology?
- Address authentic issues?

AVOID THE PITFALLS

Don't justify a project solely on the grounds that students are exercising their minds. There is sometimes a tendency to endorse the use of PBL because project work and the thinking that goes into the work appear to be intrinsically "higher-order." Students will not learn new skills from PBL unless they are challenged to do so by the conditions of the project. The tasks, behaviors, or requirements of the project should prompt students to develop new skills or construct new knowledge.

Projects versus Activity-Based Teaching Strategies

Projects are not a new instructional idea. However, well-designed projects that meet PBL criteria differ from activities, or even projects, that have been traditional in the classroom. The differences are illustrated in the table on the following page.

PROJECTS VERSUS ACTIVITY-BASED TEACHING STRATEGIES

Example Themes	Activity-Based Instruction	Project Based Learning	Differences between the Two Instructional Strategies
Civil War Battles	Take a field trip to Gettysburg. Write a report on the experience.	Investigate the question "How could wars be made more humane?" Use Gettysburg as an example of a high-casualty battle, comparing it to other battles. Complete a portfolio, including an essay and a literary response journal, then conclude with a debate.	Students investigate an overall challenging question. Distinct activities are conducted in the context of the challenge. No single activity is likely to be sufficient for responding to the challenge.
Sound Pollution	Listen to different sounds. Make a graph. Identify features of common sounds that are disturbing to the ear.	Identify five sound pollution problems in the community. Form a task force to investigate the problems and devise technically feasible solutions for each.	Although the activity-based tasks are useful for instruction, the tasks themselves may not be provocative. The project-based approach, in contrast, defines an overarching challenge and embeds these tasks (listening, graphing, identifying features) in a meaningful community project.
Ancient Architecture	Make posters depicting the architecture of ancient Egypt.	Complete a case study on the pyramids using the question "How were the pyramids built?" to address five controversial issues: source of the design, source of materials, time to completion, method of transportation of materials, and contents of the chambers.	The project addresses fundamental principles and issues. The project has an overarching question that engages students' critical thinking as well as their creativity. The project reflects current historical mysteries and investigations.
Geometry	Observe and measure various school buildings and record data.	Design a "School of the Future" with scale drawings and models, taking into account the site and anticipated needs. Present plan to an audience of school officials or community experts.	This complex project goes beyond simply "getting students out of their seats." It requires application of concepts and a defense of choices made.

6 Create the Optimal Learning Environment

Teachers can influence the success of the project by creating optimal conditions for student work. Creating or modifying the learning environment is one strategy teachers use to heighten students' interest:

- **Give your project one or more connections beyond the classroom.** One of the most powerful motivational effects of PBL can be observed when students are given authentic work to do outside of school and in collaboration with experienced partners. Possibilities include partnerships or associations with other classrooms, other schools, or the external community; electronic linkages with distant individuals, groups, or classrooms; and mentorships with community organizations.

- **Alter your classroom's look and feel.** Many PBL teachers turn their classrooms into an office or a laboratory to heighten the authenticity of the project. They partition their room to give groups private spaces to collaborate and store their work. This encourages students to take ownership of their project and can heighten student interest.

And keep in mind three ideas for improving learning in the classroom:

- **See the whole before practicing the parts.** Young children see their parents walk before their own motor skills begin to develop. Apprentices in a tailoring shop learn to assemble a garment from precut pieces before they learn to cut out the pieces themselves. In these situations, the learners see the whole before they work on the parts. Yet this is rarely the case in school. As one student said, "In school, I do little pieces of everything, but they don't really stick in my brain." Researchers say it is important for students to develop a feel for—and a conceptual map of—the overall terrain. Then, the teacher can begin to incorporate the skills and concepts necessary for expert performance and can teach students to identify conditions under which various skills and strategies apply.

- **Study content and apply it to authentic problems.** Expertise consists not only of knowing concepts, information, and procedures but also of being able to apply them to problems. At the work site, adults draw on knowledge of both content and process. However, classroom knowledge is often inert rather than dynamic; students may not develop the ability to make sense of information and think about how and when to use it.

Researchers have found that knowledge does not transfer to new situations if students do not learn problem-solving strategies and processes as well.

- **Make schoolwork more like real work.** Learning environments inside and outside of school differ in several important ways. For example, learning in school can be primarily an individual mental activity that requires little or no engagement with tools or materials. Learning outside of school often involves other people, as well as available tools and materials. Learning in school depends heavily on symbol systems that are not related to things and situations that make sense to students; outside of school, thinking and actions are grounded in the logic of immediate situations. Fred Newmann and his colleagues at the University of Wisconsin studied the way 24 schools taught mathematics and social studies.* After setting standards for teaching and learning (which had characteristics similar to those emphasized in the Six A's), the researchers found that students' scores on standardized tests and alternative assessments were higher if their classes involved work that resembled real situations.

*F. Newmann and G. Wehlage, *Successful School Restructuring: Highlights of Findings*, 1995. (Distributed by the Association for Supervision and Curriculum Development, Alexandria, Virginia.)

PROJECT IDEAS
MAPPING YOUR COMMUNITY

Adopt-a-Watershed, a national conservation organization focused on local projects in schools, uses a Community Mapping technique to develop project ideas. Below is an adapted version of that process that can be used by students to develop community-based projects. Students divide themselves into groups and ask questions about their communities. In conjunction with appropriate topics and standards in the curriculum, answers to these questions can lead to engaging, community-oriented projects. Examples of questions that students can ask about their community are:

- What are the cultures in the community?
  How many different cultures exist?
  Describe them.

- What opportunities exist for learning / teaching?

- What are the local enterprises that promote economic growth?

- What are the local community organizations?

- What celebrations take place in the community?

- What citizen actions are taking place around a critical issue?

- What are the problem areas in the community, such as noise, pollution, substandard housing, graffiti, erosion, or trash?

- What local political issues impact the community?

- What local talents exist in the community?

- What are the youth-led projects in the community?

- What are the local stories?
  Who is the most important person in the community?
  Who makes decisions?
  Who is the most respected, wisest, wealthiest, or most loved?
  How do these people connect to learning and teaching opportunities?

Continued on next page

If students interview people in the community to help answer the above questions, they can ask their fellow residents:

- What is important to them?
- What are their greatest needs?
- What environmental issues are important to them?
- Who are the important community members involved in these issues?
- What are the important relationships / partnerships?
- How would a person who wants to help with the issue best get involved?
- What is missing in what we are doing?

As a class, students can reflect on the following:

- What patterns or unexpected relations between features or systems did you observe?
- What opportunities are there for learning and teaching?
- What opportunities and resources are there to learn more about the problem / issue?
- What opportunities and resources are there to find solutions to the problem?
- Who else do we need to include to make our work most beneficial to the community?
- How will you apply your new awareness of the problem upon returning to your program?

Once the theme for a project is established, then work backwards to connect the theme to curriculum standards and design a standards-focused project.

"Mapping Your Community" is adapted from Adopt-a-Watershed.

IDENTIFYING SKILLS

The skills in the following two tables can be included as outcomes in projects.

COMMUNICATION	TECHNOLOGY	GROUP PROCESS	DESIGN
SPEAKING Persuasion, public speaking, and debating **PRESENTING** Planning and making oral presentations **WRITING** Technical writing, report writing, and expository writing **TRANSLATING** Converting information from one format to another **NOTE TAKING** Summarizing, outlining, and other study skills **PUBLISHING** Desktop publishing, using graphics, etc.	Technical literacy Using the Internet Word processing Using other software applications Using technology (telephones, computers, compasses, video cameras, and audio recorders)	Delegating and assigning roles Teamwork Listening **CONFLICT RESOLUTION** Synthesizing diverse views and using compromise and agree-to-disagree strategies **COMMUNICATION** Giving and conducting interviews, presenting to groups, reporting progress	Using a design process Planning skills and strategies Goal setting Using criteria or rubrics to guide work Using a systems approach

PROBLEM SOLVING AND CRITICAL THINKING	TASK- AND SELF-MANAGEMENT
Categorizing and analyzing Extrapolating, applying, or extending explanations Evaluating evidence or claims Evaluating value judgments Elaborating Generating ideas Generating analogies Using problem-solving strategies Brainstorming Solving problems using analogies Using search / research strategies Seeking and giving comprehensive explanations Clarifying tasks Organizing, synthesizing, and classifying information Defining and describing problems Generating hypotheses based on information Testing and evaluating hypotheses using data Drawing warranted conclusions Using decision-making strategies	**TIME MANAGEMENT** Submitting work in a timely fashion, using estimates and schedules, monitoring time, knowing how to use time efficiently, and using strategies to solve time problems **TASK MANAGEMENT** Clarifying tasks, planning, setting priorities, tracking progress, and evaluating solutions **RESOURCE MANAGEMENT (ORGANIZATION)** Following directions, keeping files, and sorting **SELF-MANAGEMENT STRATEGIES** Self-regulation, self-evaluation, self-monitoring, self-assessment, self-reinforcement, and using feedback

"Identifying Skills" is adapted from work by John Thomas.

THE SCANS SKILLS AND COMPETENCIES

The SCANS list—from the Secretary's Commission on Achieving Necessary Skills—was developed by the United States Departments of Labor and Education as a guide for educators who want to help students prepare for the workforce. The list includes five workplace competencies and a three-part foundation of skills and personal qualities needed for solid job performance.

Workplace Skills

Effective workers can productively utilize:

- **Resources**
  They know how to allocate time, money, materials, space, and staff.
- **Interpersonal Skills**
  They can work on teams, teach others, serve customers, lead, negotiate, and work well with people from culturally diverse backgrounds.
- **Information**
  They can acquire and evaluate data, organize and maintain files, interpret and communicate, and use computers to process information.
- **Systems**
  They understand social, organizational, and technological systems; they can monitor and correct performance; and they can design or improve systems.
- **Technology**
  They can select equipment and tools, apply technology to specific tasks, and maintain and troubleshoot equipment.

Foundation Competencies

Competent workers need:

- **Basic Skills**
  Reading, writing, arithmetic and mathematics, speaking and listening.
- **Thinking Skills**
  The ability to learn, reason, think creatively, make decisions, and solve problems.
- **Personal Qualities**
  Individual responsibility, self-esteem, self-management, sociability, and integrity.

"The SCANS Skills and Competencies" is adapted from What Work Requires of Schools: A SCANS Report for America 2000 *(Washington, D.C.: U.S. Department of Labor, 1991).*

THE SKILLS NECESSARY FOR SUCCESS IN THE KNOWLEDGE AGE

More ideas for skills that can be included in projects:

SEVEN C'S	COMPONENT SKILLS
Critical Thinking-and-Doing	Problem solving, research, analysis, project management, etc.
Creativity	New knowledge creation, "best fit" design solutions, artful storytelling, etc.
Collaboration	Cooperation, compromise, consensus, community-building, etc.
Cross-Cultural Understanding	Across diverse ethnic, knowledge, and organizational cultures
Communication	Crafting messages and using media effectively
Computing	Effective use of electronic information and knowledge tools
Career and Learning Self-Reliance	Managing change, lifelong learning, and career redefinition

Critical Thinking-and-Doing

Knowledge workers need to be able to define problems in complex, overlapping, ill-defined domains; use available tools and expertise, both human and electronic, for research and analysis; design promising solutions and courses of action; manage the implementations of these solutions; assess the results; and then continuously improve the solutions as conditions change.

Fluency with the design process, project management, quality management, and research methods will all be important, as well as understanding the specific content knowledge of the field involved, which will be changing dramatically and will have to be continuously refreshed "just in time." Online information databases, quick e-mail access to experts, and Web-based courses are a few of the tools that will help support this "just-in-time" learning.

Creativity

Coming up with new solutions to old problems, discovering new principles and inventing new products, creating new ways to communicate new ideas, and finding creative ways to manage complex processes and diverse teams of people will all be highly prized Knowledge Age skills.

Collaboration

Teamwork will often be the only choice for solving complex problems or for creating complex tools, services, and products—multiple talents will be essential. From coordination and collaboration to compromise and consensus, the skills for effective, collaborative teamwork will be a necessary feature of work in the Knowledge Age.

Continued on next page

Cross-Cultural Understanding

As an extension of teamwork, knowledge workers will have to bridge differing ethnic, social, organizational, political, and content knowledge cultures in order to do their work. In an increasingly multicultural society, a growing global economy, a world of increasing technical specializations, and less hierarchical organizations, cross-cultural skills will become more and more valuable.

Communication

Knowledge workers will need to be able to craft effective communications in a variety of media for a variety of audiences. Given the bewildering number of communication choices available—printed report, electronic document, magazine article, e-zine article, book, e-book, print ad, TV ad, Web ad, phone call, cell phone call, Internet phone call, voice mail, telemarketing, fax, pager, Web page, e-mail, snail mail, spreadsheet, simulation, database, multimedia presentation, slides, overheads, floppy disk, tape, video, CD, DVD, radio, TV, Web-TV, teleconferencing, virtual reality—workers will be perpetually faced with choosing the right medium for the right message for the right audience, along with the challenge of doing it all as effectively and efficiently as possible.

Computing

Everyone in the Knowledge Age will have to be able to go beyond basic computer literacy to a high level of digital fluency and comfort in using a variety of computer-based tools to accomplish the tasks of everyday life. Needless to say, those who master the knowledge tools of the Knowledge Age will be much more successful at school and at work than those who do not.

Career and Learning Self-Reliance

In an age of "at will" employment and increasing temporary and contract work, knowledge workers will have to manage their own career paths and their own continuous learning of new skills. Since most work will be high-skilled, project-based work (as opposed to low-skill service work or factory line work), the ability to manage a progressive series of shifts from one project to the next and to learn quickly what is needed to be successful in each project will all be essential to career survival and lifelong learning in the Knowledge Age.

"The Seven C's" is adapted from Bernie Trilling and Paul Hood, Educational Technology *(May / June 1999): 5–7. For more information, contact btrilli@wested.org, phood@wested.org.*

THE enGAUGE 21ST-CENTURY SKILLS

The driving force for the 21st century is the intellectual capital of citizens. Political, social, and economic advances in the United States during this millennium will be possible only if the intellectual potential of American youth is developed *now*. It should be no surprise that *what* students are learning—as well as how they learn it and *how often* they must refresh these skills sets—is changing.

The urgency to build the capacity of American workers to meet the needs of the 21st century is readily apparent in the number of high-profile groups publishing reports as "calls for action." For example, in January 2001 the National Skills Standards Board (NSSB) approved and published for public commentary the *Manufacturing Skills Standards Council Skill Standards: A Blueprint for Workforce Excellence.*

The enGauge list of 21st-century skills is compiled from many excellent works published in the 1990s, as well as contemporary literature, emerging research, and the voice of representatives from education, business, and industry. A matrix that cross-matches the enGauge skills with those of nine previous works is also available. The enGauge list is intended to provide the public, business, industry, and education with a common understanding of and language for discussing the skills needed by students and workers in this emerging Digital Age. The enGauge project is based on the premise that pre-K–12 schools should incorporate 21st-century skills and proficiencies into school curricula within the context of academic standards.

DIGITAL AGE LITERACY	INVENTIVE THINKING	EFFECTIVE COMMUNICATION	HIGH PRODUCTIVITY
Basic scientific, mathematical, and technological literacies	Adaptability and ability to manage complexity	Teaming, collaboration, and interpersonal skills	Ability to prioritize, plan, and manage for results
Visual and information literacies	Curiosity, creativity, and risk-taking	Personal and social responsibility	Effective use of real-world tools
Cultural literacy and global awareness	Higher-order thinking and sound reasoning	Interactive communication	Relevant, high-quality products

"The enGauge 21st-Century Skills" is adapted from materials provided by NCREL, North Central Regional Education Laboratory (www.ncrel.org/engauge/skills/21skills.htm).

HABITS OF MIND

What behaviors are indicative of the efficient, effective problem solver? Just what do human beings do when they behave intelligently? Research on thinking and behavior reveals some identifiable characteristics of effective thinkers. It is not necessarily scientists, artists, mathematicians, or the wealthy who demonstrate these behaviors. They have been found in mechanics, teachers, entrepreneurs, salespeople, and parents—people in all walks of life.

The following habits of mind can be included in project outcomes and assessed through self-reflection, journals, discussions, or rubrics.

Persisting

Good problem solvers stick to a task until it is completed. They don't give up easily. They are able to analyze a problem and develop a system, structure, or strategy to attack it. They have a repertoire and employ a range of alternative approaches. They collect evidence that their strategy is working, and if one strategy doesn't work, they know how to back up and try another.

Managing Impulsivity

Good problem solvers have a sense of deliberativeness. They think before they act. They intentionally form a vision of a product, a plan of action, a goal, or a destination before they begin. They strive to clarify and understand directions, develop a strategy for approaching a problem, and withhold value judgments until they fully understand an idea.

Listening to Others with Understanding and Empathy

Good problem solvers learn to devote their mental energies to listening to other speakers and thinking through their positions. We wish students to hold in abeyance their own values, judgments, opinions, and prejudices in order to entertain another person's ideas. This is a very complex skill, requiring the ability to monitor one's own thoughts while attending to someone else's words.

Thinking Flexibly

Good problem solvers are flexible thinkers and display confidence in their intuition. They tolerate confusion and ambiguity up to a point and are willing to let go of a problem, trusting their subconscious to continue creative and productive work on it.

Striving for Accuracy and Precision

Good problem solvers value accuracy, precision, and craftsmanship and take time to check over their products. They review the rules by which they are to abide, the models and visions they are to follow, and the criteria they are to employ, and they confirm that their finished product fits the criteria exactly.

Questioning and Posing Problems

Good problem solvers know how to ask questions to fill in the gaps between what they know and what they don't know. They recognize discrepancies and phenomena in their environment, probe for explanations and information, and are inclined to ask a range of questions.

Applying Past Knowledge to New Situations

Good problem solvers learn from experience. When confronted with a new and perplexing problem, they will often turn to the past for guidance. They call upon their store of knowledge and experience for sources of data and for processes that will help them solve each new challenge. Furthermore, they are able to abstract meaning from one experience, carry it forth, and apply it in new and novel situations.

Continued on next page

Gathering Data through All Senses

Good problem solvers know that information gets into the brain through all the sensory pathways: gustatory, olfactory, tactile, kinesthetic, auditory, and visual. Most linguistic, cultural, and physical learning is derived from the environment by observing or taking in through the senses.

Creating, Imagining, and Innovating

Good problem solvers have the capacity to generate novel, original, clever, or ingenious products, solutions, and techniques. Creative human beings develop that capacity, trying to conceive different problem solutions by examining alternative possibilities from many angles. They tend to project themselves into various roles using analogies.

Responding with Wonderment and Awe

Good problem solvers have not only an "I can" attitude, but also an "I enjoy" feeling. They seek challenges for themselves and others. They delight in making up problems to solve on their own, and they request enigmas from others. They enjoy figuring things out by themselves and continue to learn throughout their lifetimes.

Taking Responsible Risks

Good problem solvers tend to go beyond established limits; they "live on the edge" of their competence. They accept confusion, uncertainty, and the higher risks of failure as part of the norm, and they view setbacks as interesting, challenging, and growth-producing. However, they do not behave impulsively. Their risks are calculated. They draw on past knowledge, are thoughtful about consequences, and have a well-trained sense of which risks are worthwhile.

Finding Humor

Good problem solvers can laugh at themselves. Laughter is universal medicine. Its positive effects on physiological functions include a drop in the pulse rate, the secretion of endorphins, and increased oxygen in the blood. It has been found to liberate creativity and provoke such high-level thinking skills as anticipating, finding novel relationships, using visual imagery, and making analogies.

Thinking Interdependently

Good problem solvers realize that all of us together are more powerful, intellectually and physically, than any one individual. We find ourselves increasingly more interdependent and sensitive to others' needs. Problem solving has become so complex that no one has access to all the data needed to make critical decisions; no one person can consider as many alternatives as several people can.

Learning Continuously

Good problem solvers are continually learning. Their confidence, in combination with their inquisitiveness, allows them to constantly search for new and better methods. People with this habit of mind are always striving for improvement, always growing, always learning, always modifying and improving themselves. They seize problems, situations, tensions, conflicts, and circumstances as valuable opportunities to learn.

"Habits of Mind" is adapted from A. L. Costa and B. Kallick, eds., Discovering and Exploring Habits of Mind *(Alexandria, Virginia: Association for Supervision and Curriculum Development, 2000).*

THE SIX A'S—CRITERIA FOR DESIGNING PROJECTS

This list of questions, derived from Adria Steinberg's synthesis in her book, *Real Learning, Real Work*, provides a framework used by Jobs for the Future in working with teachers as they plan curricular projects.

Authenticity

- Where in the "real world" might an adult tackle the problem or question addressed by the project?
- How do you know the problem or question has meaning to the students?
- Who might be appropriate audiences for the students' work?

Academic Rigor

- What is the central problem or question addressed by the project?
- What knowledge area and central concepts will it address?
- What habits of mind will students develop? (e.g., questioning and posing problems; precision of language and thought; persistence)
- What learning standards are you addressing through this project? Cite the source, e.g., district or state.

Applied Learning

- What will the students do to apply the knowledge they are learning to a complex problem? Are they designing a product, improving a system, organizing an event?
- Which of the competencies expected in high-performance work organizations (e.g., working in teams; using technology appropriately; communicating ideas; collecting, organizing, and analyzing information) does the project provide opportunities to develop?
- Which self-management skills (e.g., developing a work plan, prioritizing pieces of work, meeting deadlines, identifying and allocating resources) does the project require students to use?

Active Exploration

- What field-based activities does the project require students to conduct? (e.g., interviewing expert(s) or participating in a worksite exploration)

Continued on next page

Active Exploration, *Continued*

- Which methods and sources of information are students expected to use in their investigations? (e.g., interviewing and observing, gathering and reviewing information, collecting data, model-building, using on-line services)

Adult Connections

- Do students have access to at least one outside adult with expertise and experience relevant to their project who can ask questions, provide feedback, and offer advice?
- Does the project offer students the opportunity to observe and work alongside adults during at least one visit to a worksite with relevance to the project?
- Does at least one adult from outside the classroom help students develop a sense of the real-world standards for this type of work?

Assessment Practices

- What are the criteria for measuring desired student outcomes (disciplinary knowledge, habits of mind, and applied learning goals)?
- Are students involved in reviewing or helping to establish the project criteria?
- Which methods of structured self-assessment are students expected to use? (e.g., journals, peer conferences, teacher or mentor conferences, rubrics, periodic review of progress vis-à-vis the work plan)
- Do students receive timely feedback on their works-in-progress from teachers, mentors, and peers?
- What work requirements are students expected to complete during the life of the project? (e.g., proposal, work plan, reflection paper, mini-presentation, models, illustrations)
- Do students prepare a culminating exhibition or presentation at the completion of the project that demonstrates their ability to apply the knowledge they have gained?

On the next page is a rubric that can be used by you and your project team to evaluate the design of projects based on the Six A's.

"The Six A's" is adapted from Adria Steinberg, Real Learning, Real Work *(Boston, Massachusetts: Jobs for the Future, 1997). The rubric is adapted from materials provided by Napa New Technology High School, Napa, California.*

Rubric for the Six A's

CATEGORY	UNSATISFACTORY	BASIC	EXEMPLARY
Authenticity	• The project has little or no connection with the outside world. • The problem or question has little or no meaning to the students. • There is no audience for the student work.	• The project simulates "real world" activities. • The problem or question has meaning to the students. • There is an appropriate audience for the student work.	• Adults in the "real world" are likely to tackle the problem or questions addressed by the project. • The problem or question has meaning to the students. • There is an external audience for the student work.
Academic Rigor	• The Driving Question is not based on standards. • The project demands little specific knowledge of central concepts. • Students can complete the project without learning new content. • Project does not include habits of mind in outcomes.	• The Driving Question is based on standards. • The project demands specific knowledge of central concepts. • Students learn minimal content. • Project reinforces previously learned habits of mind.	• There is a well-defined and clear Driving Question that is derived from specific national, state, district, or school content standards. • The project demands breadth and depth of specific knowledge of central concepts. • Students develop new habits of mind (e.g., questioning and posing problems; precision of language and thought; persistence).
Applied Learning	• Students do not apply new knowledge to a problem. • Students are not required to develop collaborative or teamwork skills.	• Students apply new knowledge to a problem. • Students are required to work in teams. • Students use self-management skills to improve their performance.	• Students apply new knowledge to a realistic and complex problem. • Students use multiple high-performance work organization skills (e.g., working in teams; using technology appropriately; communicating ideas, collecting, organizing, and analyzing information). • Students formally use self-management skills (e.g., developing a work plan, prioritizing pieces of work, meeting deadlines, identifying and allocating resources) to improve their team's performance.
Active Exploration	• No research is required. • Students gather information from textbooks or other secondary sources. • Students use raw data provided by the teacher.	• Students conduct their own research. • Students gather information from a limited number of primary sources.	• Students do field-based activities (e.g., interviewing experts, surveying groups of people, exploring worksites). • Students gather information from a variety of primary sources and use a variety of methods (interviewing and observing, collecting data, model-building, using on-line services).
Adult Connections	• Students have no contacts with adults outside of school.	• Students have limited contacts with adults outside of school (e.g., guest speakers). • The teacher uses role-playing or other staff members to simulate "expert" contact.	• Students have multiple contacts with adults outside of school who have expertise and experience and who can ask questions, provide feedback, and offer advice. • Students have the opportunity to observe and work alongside adults in a worksite relevant to the project. • Adults outside of school provide students with a sense of the real-world standards for this type of work.
Assessment Practices	• Students are not provided with explanation of the assessment at early stages of the assignment. • The only product is a culminating exhibition or presentation.	• Students are provided with a clear explanation of the assessment in the early stages of this assignment. • Students receive infrequent feedback on their works-in-progress from teachers, mentors, and peers. • The project includes multiple products. • The final product is a culminating exhibition or presentation that demonstrates their ability to apply the knowledge they have gained.	• Students help in establishing assessment criteria. • Students use a variety of structured self-assessments (journals, peer conferences, teacher or mentor conferences, rubrics). • Students receive frequent and timely feedback on their works-in-progress from teachers, mentors, and peers. • The final product is a culminating exhibition or presentation in front of an informed audience. • The project employs multiple products, and all products are aligned with outcomes.

BEGIN WITH
THE END
IN MIND

CRAFT THE
DRIVING QUESTION

PLAN THE
ASSESSMENT

Designing
and
Planning
Successful
Projects

MAP THE
PROJECT

MANAGE
THE
PROCESS

Contents

IDEA BANK

CRAFT THE DRIVING QUESTION

Here, you will learn about a critical task: distilling the theme and content standards into a significant, meaningful question that engages students and helps them focus their efforts throughout the project.

In this section, you will learn how to craft and refine the Driving Question. A good Driving Question makes a project intriguing, complex, and problematic. Although standard classroom assignments like story problems and essays pose questions that students must answer, a Driving Question requires multiple activities and the synthesis of different types of information before it can be answered. It brings coherence to disparate project activities and serves as a "lighthouse" that promotes student interest and directs students toward the project's goals and objectives. Also, Driving Questions should address authentic concerns. For example, when creating the Driving Question it is useful to ask yourself: "Where is the content I am trying to teach used in the real world?" Although it is usually easier to focus students' attention on a single question, some topics will require multiple Driving Questions.

GUIDELINES FOR THE DRIVING QUESTION

Once you have a project theme or a "big idea" for a project, capture the theme in the form of a problem or a question that cannot be easily solved or answered. For example, if your big idea is the potential danger of global warming, develop a question such as "Should we be worried about global warming in our community?" Developing a question is a process that can be done with students. Examples of Driving Questions for various subjects can be found in the **Idea Bank**.

When creating the Driving Question, use the following guidelines:

- **Driving Questions are provocative.**
  They must sustain students' interest during the project and challenge students to go beyond superficialities.

  Do music videos paint an accurate picture of America? This question not only compels students to focus on culture in America and media portrayals, but it is also a provocative question that will engage teenagers.

- **Driving Questions are open-ended.**
  They do not lead to easy answers. Instead, Driving Questions engage students in

AVOID THE PITFALLS

Driving Questions to Avoid
Driving Questions should be open-ended, but also feasible. They must be conceived with an eye toward available time, resources, and student skills. For example, a question such as "Who was the most effective president in the 20th century?" is provocative but requires detailed research. It may not be possible to adequately answer the question in the scope of a typical project.

higher-level thinking and require them to integrate, synthesize, and critically evaluate information. Make sure the question cannot be answered with a simple "yes" or "no."

Should the United States have used the atomic bomb in World War II? This question requires a deep examination of the arguments in favor of or against dropping the bomb. The question is open-ended; it allows students to consider the arguments and come up with their own answer, based on their own reasoning and logic.

- **Driving Questions go to the heart of a discipline or topic.** They can focus on controversies central to a field and debated by the professionals within them.

How safe is our water? That Driving Question, used in the Shutesbury Water Project described later in the **Project Examples** section of the Handbook, requires scientific evidence and professional judgments based on criteria developed in biology, chemistry, and physiology. To answer the question, students must investigate and learn the criteria used in scientific fields.

- **Driving Questions are challenging.** They encourage students to confront difficult issues and try out unfamiliar behaviors.

When are people justified in revolting against an established government? This Driving Question was developed by a 12th-grade history teacher for a project designed to address national standards associated with conflict and revolution, as well as historical inquiry. Students studied revolutions and revolutionary movements in Central America, Russia, Spain, and Africa, looking for common patterns and principles.

- **Driving Questions can arise from real-world dilemmas that students find interesting.**

How could we build a new community center using only materials that are native to the state? A Vermont science teacher wanted her students to understand how rocks are formed and to learn about the sources, properties, and mineral compositions of indigenous Vermont rocks. This Driving Question focused students' attention on identifying the structural elements and features of a community center and evaluating the strength and durability of natural and manufactured materials available in the state. More important, the Driving Question led students to

---

AVOID THE PITFALLS

Beware of bells and whistles. All project activities should be designed to help answer the Driving Question. But too often, the use of technological tools in a project obscures the problem-solving process. Technology becomes the focus of a project—and students are then evaluated on their use of technology rather than on their conclusions or evidence regarding the Driving Question.

---

make careful decisions about why, for example, slate is appropriate for roofs, but not for playgrounds.

- **Driving Questions are consistent with curricular standards and frameworks.** It is not enough for a question to be provocative. It must also lead students to master the agreed-upon skills, knowledge, and processes that define a course of study. *Should the United States develop the capability for biological warfare?* That's a provocative question, but not one that is directly related to United States history or American government standards. Be sure that Driving Questions pull students in the direction of learning the essential standards.

REFINING THE DRIVING QUESTION

Creating a powerful Driving Question usually involves drafting and refining the first version of the question. Questions must often be enriched to require students to grapple with a complex issue, engage the big ideas, learn content standards, and "do" as well as "know." Here are examples of how questions can be improved:

REFINING THE DRIVING QUESTION

Was Truman's decision to drop the bomb justified?	➤	**Can the use of nuclear weapons be justified?**
Powerful question. It forces students to confront the dilemmas of war. Students will not only learn history, but they will also learn about issues that remain relevant today.		Broadening the question can increase its power. If time is available, the project can now focus on a number of different decisions about the use of nuclear force, require students to compare these situations, and lead students to develop and justify their own decision criteria.
How have robotics and automation changed our society in the past century?	➤	**How might robotics and automation change our town and its businesses in the next century?**
Good question. The question prompts students to learn about economics and automation, and it also leads students to apply what they have learned.		A better question. Students will need to learn how society has changed to date from automation and robotics. They might also learn about anticipated technological changes and their possible effects, and they are sure to find this project more engaging.

What happened to the ancestral Pueblo people? Create an exhibit using words and pictures.

The question prompts students to learn what life was like in pre-Columbian America and appeals to their interest in mysterious phenomena. However, this is a question that has not yet been answered by adults or experts.

➤ **Why do civilizations such as the ancestral Pueblo, Inca, or Aztec civilizations disappear? Put together a presentation suitable for an archeology convention that supports your case.**

A better question. Examining multiple civilizations for common themes and including expert guidelines for a presentation can increase students' learning of pre-Columbian civilizations.

What is global warming?

Good beginning. The topic is central to both the earth science curriculum and current events.

➤ **Should we be worried about global warming in our town?**

This rewording brings the Driving Question home. With this statement, students can anchor their investigations in local geography, climate, and ecosystems.

What have been the most popular novels among teenagers in the last 30 years?

Good beginning. The question integrates the curriculum topics of genres, plots, and characters in a way that teenagers might find appealing.

➤ **How has reading changed for teenagers over the last 30 years?**

Good reframing. This question covers the same content as the initial question, but it adds a challenging element to the project.

What is radiation fog and how can it be dangerous?

Good beginning. The question requires students to focus on central scientific principles.

➤ **How can we reduce traffic accidents associated with radiation fog?**

Good expansion to a problem-based framework. Students will have to understand the principles of radiation fog and also apply this understanding to generate solutions.

EXAMPLES OF DRIVING QUESTIONS

These are examples of *possible* Driving Questions. Use them if they fit with appropriate content standards and project outcomes.

History

- Who are we and how did we get here?
- Has the importance of the individual increased over time?
- Are freedom and democracy spreading around the world?
- What is the price of "progress"?
- Are wars avoidable?
- How are wars won?
- Could the British have avoided the revolution in the American colonies?
- Was the American Revolution really a revolution?
- What effects does the Civil War still have on us today?
- Should African Americans receive reparations for slavery?
- How did the United States become a world power?
- What were the lessons of Vietnam?
- Who were the best leaders of the 20th century?
- How can we bring peace to the Middle East?
- How has 18th- and 19th-century European colonization affected 21st-century Africa?
- Will China be the next superpower?

Humanities / Interdisciplinary (History / English)

- What is the American Dream and who has it?
- How do immigrants meet the challenges of coming to a new country?
- Do victors really benefit from winning wars?
- How do we make peace?
- Can the use of nuclear weapons be justified?
- How should we respond to terrorism?

English

- Why is Shakespeare still so popular?
- Why are books banned?
- What is "good writing"?
- How can someone overcome adversity?
- What makes a book a "classic"?
- What does it mean to "come of age"?
- What is friendship (love, hatred, loyalty, courage, etc.)?
- How do we persuade others?
- Which novels belong in a high school curriculum?
- How does literature reflect the times in which it is written?

Art

- Why do we make art?
- What makes a good artist? A great one?
- How does art reflect its time?
- Is art worth its price?
- Should there be censorship?

Geography

- How does the place we live in affect how we live?
- How do human actions modify the physical environment?
- How can we use geography to interpret the past?

Continued on next page

Economics

- Why do things cost so much?
- What is necessary to run a successful business?
- What is the best investment to make with your money?
- What's your money worth now and in the future?
- Why is there poverty?

- Should natural resources be used or protected?
- Who has economic power in America?
- How should international trade be conducted?
- What should be the government's role in regulating the economy?

Government

- Do we have too much freedom?
- What is the right balance between security and freedom?
- What is the best form of government?
- Who has power in this country?
- What are our rights and duties as citizens?
- How much power does the President have?

- Why has the United States Constitution lasted so long?
- Should the Bill of Rights be revised?
- What should be the goals of United States foreign policy?
- How should criminals be treated?
- What should local government do about (insert various possible topics: poverty, homelessness, the use of land, improving services, etc.)?

The Driving Questions for many projects in science and math can be based on solving a problem, i.e., Problem Based Learning, in which students are presented with authentic problems requiring the application of scientific knowledge, understanding, concepts, and skills.

Science

- What is the earth made of?
- What are we made of?
- How will the land we live on change over time?
- What is light?
- Can we predict the weather?
- Should we be concerned about global warming in our community?
- How good is our water?
- How do amusement park rides work?
- Are amusement park rides safe?

- How should a bridge be designed for this site?
- How can we use the laws of physics to predict the motion of a flying object so that we can design an entertaining fireworks display?
- How can we use Newton's three laws to create a sport that takes advantage of the unique characteristics of the moon?
- How can we stop the spread of an infectious disease?
- How can endangered species be saved?
- Should we produce genetically engineered foods?
- Do we have anything to fear from electromagnetic fields?

Math

- What is the best design for a ''high school of the future'' for a given site?
- How can we describe the shape of a rocket's flight?
- Is it better to buy or lease a car?
- How should a tax form be done?
- Can we predict the level of activity on our Website?
- How can we use the principles of probability to assess the state lottery system?

- What effect does rapid population growth have on our society, and how can we analyze and model this growth mathematically?
- Can we predict the growth of a Website's use?
- How can we experimentally and mathematically model a landing sequence like that of the Pathfinder mission?
- How can hikers determine the shortest distance between two points?
- How can we predict the motion of a flying object to design a fireworks show?

BEGIN WITH
THE END
IN MIND

Designing
and
Planning
Successful
Projects

CRAFT THE
DRIVING
QUESTION

PLAN
THE ASSESSMENT

MAP THE
PROJECT

MANAGE
THE
PROCESS

Contents

Every project should be driven by an explicit set of outcomes that encompass the key content, skills, and habits of mind that students are expected to learn. In this section, you will learn how to develop multiple products that give all students opportunities to demonstrate their learning and that form the basis for a balanced assessment plan for the project. You will also learn to develop rubrics.

IDEA BANK

PLAN THE ASSESSMENT

roject Based Learning reorients learners and teachers away from traditional paper and pencil tests and toward more "authentic" assessment practices. In addition to teaching content, instructional goals associated with PBL are tied to the *use* of knowledge and skills as students go about a problem-solving activity. This calls for performance assessments that evaluate the skills necessary for higher-order thinking, the tasks required for students to produce a quality product, and the method of disciplined inquiry through which students integrate content and process to produce useful knowledge.

Since they are aimed at measuring authentic practices such as collaboration, communication, problem solving, and teamwork, performance-based assessments are more diverse than traditional assessments. These practices are dynamic, experiential, and nonstandardized, requiring assessments that can capture the process of learning, as well as the end result.

CREATING A BALANCED ASSESSMENT PLAN

In the real world of teaching, you are responsible for all kinds of learning. Students need to know the content of the subject; they also need to know how to apply it. Teachers must choose the right assessment for the right product and decide which blend of assessments will provide evidence that students have met the range of outcomes for the project. Tests and traditional research papers or essays can be easily integrated into PBL. At the same time, projects must include assessments that capture the process-oriented outcomes of PBL. Often, the products from a project are designed to accomplish both goals—to measure content knowledge as well as skills.

A balanced assessment plan for a project will include a variety of assessments closely tied to the outcomes—the content standards, skills, and habits of mind—of the project. Most important, multiple indicators for performance give different kinds of students, each with different strengths, the opportunity to succeed.

A balanced assessment plan also includes methods you will use to gather the evidence of student performance, interpret that evidence, and make judgments about the evidence. The assessment plan should include both *formative* assessments—assessments that allow you to

PLAN THE ASSESSMENT

45

give feedback as the project progresses—and *summative* assessments —assessments that provide students with a culminating appraisal of their performance.

1 Align Products with Outcomes

Once the outcomes for the project have been decided, planning effective assessments requires that you work backwards to *align the products or performances for the project with the outcomes.* Products are the presentations, papers, exhibits, or models that are completed during a project. What products will provide adequate evidence of student learning and achievement? Every outcome must be assessed, giving students the opportunity through their products to demonstrate what they are required to know and do. This step includes:

- Identifying *culminating products* for a project.
- Using *multiple products* and a checkpoint system for feedback to students.
- Using *artifacts*—evidence of the process of student thinking—to assess skills and habits of mind.

> Planning effective assessments requires that you work backwards to align the products or performances for the project with the outcomes.

After deciding on the products, you must then *establish performance criteria* to assess each product or performance, including:

- *"Unpacking"* content standards and skills.
- Writing *rubrics.*

This process will help you devise an assessment plan that is fair and accurate, targets specific content and skills, and provides timely, useful feedback to students. At the end of the project, you will be able to answer three important questions: (1) how well do the students know the content? (2) what is their skill level? and (3) how well did they apply their knowledge and skills as they prepared their products?

Working Backwards—How Will Products Allow Students to Demonstrate Their Learning?

As an example, let us assume that your project asks students to demonstrate proficiency in three areas: (1) two academic content standards; (2) oral presentation and research skills; and (3) the habit of mind of reflection. Each outcome must be assessed and included in one or more of the components of the products for the project. First, you might decide that students will produce:

- An exhibition such as a video or oral presentation that requires them to demonstrate knowledge of the subject based on the content standards and presentation skills.
- A research paper on a topic encompassed by the content standards.
- A journal that records their progress during the project.

Assessing the quality of student work in these products requires different methods. The presentation and the research paper can be assessed using a performance rubric. Journals can be assessed formally or informally. Additional content outcomes can also be assessed through an exam. You now have the basis for creating an effective assessment plan using a culminating product, multiple products, and artifacts.

Culminating Products

A *culminating* product is due at the end of the project and often represents a blend of content knowledge and skills that give students an opportunity to demonstrate learning across a variety of topics and skills. Culminating products are often presented during significant, high-stakes occasions involving audiences beyond the classroom, thus encouraging students to go beyond "show-and-tell" and to demonstrate in-depth learning.

Examples of culminating products include:

- **Research papers.** A culminating product can be a traditional essay or research paper.
- **Reports.** Students investigating a major issue in a project may conduct an analysis or do research on an important societal or community question. This can culminate in a report to the community or to the school.
- **Multimedia shows.** Using digital media, students can create an electronic presentation that can be included in an on-line portfolio or shown at an exhibition.
- **Presentations within the school.** Presentations or demonstrations to school-wide assemblies or other classrooms are

effective environments for increasing the quality of student performances. If it is possible, you should avoid having students present only to members of their own class.

- **Exhibitions outside of school.** Presentations to parents and community members can consist of oral presentations or presentation of an art or media project.

EXHIBITIONS

Exhibitions are one type of product in which students have the opportunity to show their work and report on what they have learned. Examples of exhibitions include performances, portfolio defenses, presentations, displays, and student-led events at fairs and shows.

Exhibitions lend themselves to multiple assessment methods. Content knowledge, for example, can be assessed on the basis of a single student performance and the portfolio of work on which the performance is based. Post-exhibition self-reports allow students to explain how their thinking changed as a result of their participation.

Exhibitions have a number of advantages as a way to conclude a project:

- Students can help plan exhibitions and establish the criteria by which they will be judged. In this way, preparation for the exhibition can become as important as the event itself.
- Multiple exhibitions over time enable students to demonstrate their progress toward different goals or criteria.
- Students can prepare their exhibitions with others and receive emotional support and feedback.
- Exhibitions are good exercises in meta-cognitive training (e.g., planning, goal setting, self-monitoring, knowing when to seek help, keeping to a schedule, etc.).
- Exhibitions are settings in which students are treated as knowledgeable practitioners who have information to share with others.
- Exhibitions involve others in student assessment. The teacher's assessment of student learning can be supplemented by peer assessment, evaluation by local experts, student self-assessment, and the judgment of parents and other community members. Students and others can develop assessment criteria or a rubric, provide feedback as students practice their performances, judge products, or assess culminating performances.

Multiple Products

Multiple products are due during the early, middle, or late stages of the project. Multiple products can include preliminary and culminating products and can be produced by individuals and/or groups.

Using multiple products has distinct advantages. First, the use of multiple products in conjunction with early and mid-project milestones gives students more opportunities to improve over time and meet the project outcomes. Multiple products give you as a teacher more control over the process, providing you an early look at whether students are meeting the goals of the project or encountering unforeseen problems. They also provide for specific content checkpoints at which students (and the teacher) can assess student progress, decide on alternative directions, and make realistic estimates of the amount of time necessary for project completion. These checkpoints may also include quizzes, short assignments, or tests.

Second, multiple products offer students multiple opportunities to demonstrate their learning and proficiencies. Using multiple products to organize a systematic set of checkpoints for project products will not only help keep students on schedule, but it will also help them refine and improve their work.

A systematic set of checkpoints for project products will not only help keep students on schedule, but it will also help them refine and improve their work.

The art of designing a project requires that activities and products be carefully planned. Each activity should yield information and build the skills that will result in a successful product. Then, at key points in the process, a product should be collected from students and evaluated. For example, a research paper based on interviews may be a culminating product for a project. But the paper requires that students know how to conduct a formal interview and organize the results of the interview. This is an activity, but it may result in an interview plan—another product for the project.

Examples of multiple products include:

Proposals	Edited drafts	Final versions
Outlines	Revised drafts	of papers
Plans	Models	Field guides
Blueprints	Product critiques	Biographies
Drafts	Videos	Websites

Artifacts

Active learning is one of the goals of PBL, which can introduce challenging class management issues. But the power of effective PBL design lies in the ability of projects to pull students through the curriculum by engaging them in complex, relevant problem solving. The problem-solving process is inherently ambiguous, with a creative stage in which students investigate, think, reflect, draft, and test hypotheses. Much of this work takes place in a collaborative mode, which can be noisy and disordered. The value of this process is that *this is the way the world works.* Helping students produce quality work through this process is invaluable to their lives. The best way to assist them is to guide them through the process with a set of tools and evaluate the methods they are using to go about the process. Then discuss your evaluation with students. In this way, the process itself is part of the content of the project.

How do you capture this process for evaluation and assessment? Look for *artifacts* of the process—the evidence that the process of planning, questioning, and problem solving has occurred. Artifacts can be used to evaluate both skills and habits of mind. They require the same considerations as other products—that is, you must establish and share with students the standards and expectations for the artifacts. Some of the evidence collected from the process can be easily graded; other pieces of evidence are more informal and will give you a feel for how the students are doing. All of this evidence is useful when offered as constructive feedback to students. Creating artifacts also encourages the skill of record keeping, an important skill in life and in the work world.

Examples of artifacts include:
> Notes
> Journal entries
> E-mail records
> Records of conversations, decisions, and revisions
> Interviews using a structured set of questions
> Short reflective paragraphs describing the progress of a project

Additional examples are in the **Idea Bank**.

AVOID THE PITFALLS

Don't dumb down the task. To create a project where every student can perform every task will require limiting project demands to those that can be met by the least able student. Such dumbing down of the task can limit the challenge of the project, restrict the range of learning that might emerge, and shortcut the possibility that less able students might learn from their more able peers. Let students help set their own limits and challenges.

2 Know What to Assess

Content knowledge and skills need to be broken down—unpacked and laid out in a series of specific statements of what needs to be learned. These statements become the basis for the assessment process and provide guidance to students on what they should learn. Often, the benchmarks for standards serve this purpose. But you may want to add your own key points under each benchmark, to give students an exact idea of what they need to do.

As an example of unpacking the task, think of an oral presentation. A presentation includes at least three subskills: eye contact, physical posture, and voice projection. It may also include other elements, such as having an engaging opening, offering a coherent argument, or including certain key facts and vocabulary related to the content of the presentation.

Similarly, habits of mind—even such qualities as perseverance or flexibility—can be defined by specific statements or indicators. For example, the number of resources used in a research paper or the number of sites searched during a Web-based project provides some evidence that a student persevered throughout a project.

3 Use Rubrics

The outcomes in projects are both content-driven and performance-oriented. PBL therefore requires assessments that effectively measure academic achievement and the application of knowledge. For those reasons, rubrics are essential to PBL.

A rubric is a scoring guide that clearly differentiates levels of student performance. When written well, rubrics provide a clear description of proficient student work and serve as a guide for helping students achieve and exceed performance standards. From the students' standpoint, the most pertinent fact about rubrics is that they are not secret. From the outset of a project, rubrics should be available to students, and they may be able to help create rubrics.

Rubrics are an excellent organizing tool for a project. The process of writing a rubric requires teachers to think deeply about what they want their students to know and do.

Rubrics work best when accompanied by exemplars, and it is useful to provide opportunities for students to apply rubrics to samples of previous student work before the project begins. Students then know exactly the standard they are expected to achieve, as well as the specific indicators of achievement that must be mastered for proficiency. Using this anchoring process, students and teachers will have a common interpretation of the language in the rubric. This facilitates your goal of helping all students achieve a standard of performance, rather than sorting out students through a surprise process that reveals who "got it" and who didn't.

For teachers, rubrics are an excellent organizing tool for a project. The process of writing a rubric requires teachers to think deeply about what they want their students to know and do. The clearer the outcomes, the clearer the assignments and the better the products.

The Central Features of Effective Rubrics

Rubrics recommended for use in the classroom are *analytic* rubrics, which break down the tasks in an assignment into separate categories for assessment. For example, an analytic rubric for a research paper might contain criteria for five categories: (1) content; (2) organization; (3) depth of research; (4) use of primary resources; and (5) writing mechanics. This breakdown allows teachers to facilitate student learning during the project by giving students more specific feedback. Analytic rubrics do not combine independent tasks in one criteria.

Holistic rubrics use multiple criteria, but they combine the criteria to arrive at a single score. For example, the criteria for an oral presentation may include eye contact with the audience, body posture, use of notes, and delivery. These would be scored as a whole, with one overall score. Though useful for certain tasks, such as a quick overall evaluation of a proposal or project, holistic rubrics lack the detail that is useful to students.

In general, effective rubrics:

- Are based on an analysis of student work. As the number of work samples that are evaluated increases, so does the validity and reliability of the rubric.
- Discriminate among performances by targeting the central features of performance, instead of the features that are the easiest to see, count, or score.
- Provide useful and apt discrimination to enable sufficiently fine judgments, but not by using so many points on a scale as to make it impossible to decide between categories of performance.

- Use descriptors that are sufficiently rich to enable students to verify their score, accurately self-assess, and self-correct.
- Provide indicators that are less ambiguous and more reliable by giving examples of what to look for in recognizing each level of performance, rather than relying on descriptive language that uses comparatives or value language (e.g., "not as thorough as" or "excellent product") to make the discriminations.

School-Wide Rubrics

If your school presents the opportunity, writing school-wide rubrics that apply throughout grade levels and subjects can be a powerful tool for developing high standards of achievement in your school community. For example, through staff agreements, school-wide rubrics can be established for writing, oral presentations, collaboration, critical thinking, and problem solving. School-wide rubrics can also be written to encourage habits of mind associated with outcomes such as promoting tolerance, curiosity, and respect.

Guidelines for Writing Rubrics

Rubrics can be written for virtually any task or product. Separate rubrics can be created for content and skills, but rubrics often are designed to assess both content and skills for a product. Rubrics may be written to assess collaboration in groups, or individual performances. Most important, *each major product* in a project requires a rubric.

The use of rubrics increases the students' sense of fairness about grading and reduces quibbling over grades.

Writing rubrics is one of the most challenging tasks facing teachers. To write clear descriptions of proficient student work requires thoughtful analysis, drafting and redrafting, and piloting. But the payoff is substantial. The use of rubrics increases the students' sense of fairness about grading and reduces quibbling over grades. Rubrics acknowledge the subjectivity of grading, while at the same time providing a more precise, objective tool for feedback. Even if you struggle with writing rubrics, students will appreciate your efforts to enhance the learning and assessment process.

All rubrics share three common features: elements, scales, and criteria.

ELEMENTS*

Any performance or product can be broken down into a set of elements, or individual components. These elements describe various aspects of a product and become the framework for the rubric. For example, the elements below describe five different ways to evaluate a presentation of an idea or a product. These five elements can be listed on the rubric to provide a comprehensive description of performance:

- **Impact of performance**. The success of performance, given the purposes, goals, and desired result.
- **Work quality and craftsmanship**. The overall polish, organization, and rigor of the work.
- **Adequacy of methods and behaviors**. The quality of the procedures and manner of presentation, prior to and during performance.
- **Validity of content**. The correctness of the ideas, skills, or materials used.
- **Sophistication of knowledge employed**. The complexity or maturity of the knowledge displayed.

SCALES

A scale that describes the level of performance, such as "Basic," "Proficient," and "Advanced," must accompany each element of a rubric. Most rubrics use three-point, four-point, five-point, or six-point scales. The number of points is a matter of personal preference and also depends on the product to be evaluated. More complex products may require larger scales to discriminate between the levels of performance. It is useful to remember that rubrics with even-numbered scales can be slightly more difficult to score, since odd-numbered rubrics more easily accommodate an "average" score (e.g., a score of three on a five-point scale).

Points to remember when building your rubric include:
- The language used to label the scale should reflect performance in relation to standards ("below standard," "approaches standard," "meets standard," "exceeds standard").
- Use enough points on the scale so that the degrees of student performance can be accurately represented.

*These sections are adapted from work by Grant Wiggins.

CRITERIA

Criteria are specific descriptors used to determine success, or degree of success, at meeting a goal or outcome. Examples of criteria, in relation to performance goals, are:

- Criteria for running a one-mile race—finish the race in less than four minutes.
- Criteria for an effective oral presentation—maintain eye contact with audience members during 80 percent of the presentation.
- Criteria for collaborating effectively—each member of the group makes a visible or meaningful contribution to the final product.

To apply criteria to the elements and scales in a rubric, you must:

- Decide which criteria apply to different aspects of performance (impact of performance, work quality and craftsmanship, adequacy of methods and behaviors, validity of content, and sophistication of knowledge employed).
- Write criteria that describe behaviors or results that you can measure or easily observe. If the aim is "effective writing," then the criteria might be *engaging, mindful of audience, clear, focused, effective voice, etc.*
- Decide which criteria are critical for this particular assignment. Too many criteria are difficult to assess thoroughly.
- Always build your rubrics from the top, starting from a description of exemplary performance. Regardless of whether or not students can perform at exemplary levels, the rubric must be built from a picture of excellence to establish a valid target and anchor for the scoring. If available, use top student work to help build the picture of outstanding performance, or use the work of professionals.

Regardless of whether or not students can perform at exemplary levels, the rubric must be built from a picture of excellence to establish a valid target and anchor for the scoring.

A descriptor or indicator contains concrete language that identifies typical behaviors, traits, or signs of performance related to the criteria. The key to developing good descriptors and indicators is to amplify the meaning of words like "excellent" with language that describes what excellence actually looks like in performance. Again, use student work to build the rubric and increase the validity and clarity of language.

Additional Tips

There are other tricks to writing good rubrics. You may find the following helpful:

- **Use Bloom's Taxonomy.** The language of rubrics is important. For examples of language, look at the verbs in Bloom's Taxonomy (see the **Idea Bank** in this section). These active verbs lend themselves to ideas on how students can demonstrate proficiencies in key processes of learning.

- **Link the scoring criteria to content standards.** One excellent way to design a rubric is to consult the benchmarks or indicators for the content standards that are part of the outcomes for the projects. Using that language guarantees that students will be assessed on vital content.

- **Find the right number of rubrics and level of specificity.** Projects can end up with too many rubrics, which is confusing to both students and teachers. On the other hand, too few rubrics do not allow for adequate assessment on major projects. Deciding how many rubrics to use can be a challenge because every task can be broken down into a subtask, another subtask, and so on. The challenge is to decide the essential elements that you want to assess and the proper level of specificity.

- **Use student language.** To facilitate understanding, teachers often have students rewrite standards in their own language. This can also be done with rubrics. Alternatively, students themselves can design rubrics and write the language for the rubrics. This process works particularly well when students focus on the highest standards and create language for exemplary products. This helps students internalize the goals and standards for the project.

- **Maintain a high standard for exemplary work.** The best work should be *very* good, so that students have a worthy target. Using exemplary descriptions based on high standards allows you to build a complete rubric with more nuance and breadth of language. Of course, performance levels also must be calibrated to the level of achievement of your students. Rubrics may change as students change and master new skills and content. Either rubrics can be rewritten to keep pace with improving skills, or the weight of sections in the rubric can change to emphasize different skills.

- **Judge the product, rather than guess at the process.** Avoid language in the rubric that makes you guess whether something happened. Rather, focus on the tangible results. For example, instead of a rubric descriptor that describes students as "showing *insight*" into a problem, focus on the product of the problem-solving or creative process.

Refer to the **Idea Bank** after this section for examples of rubrics. These are the best guides to designing rubrics for your project.

Rubrics and Grades

Several solutions are available if you would like to integrate your current grading system with performance-based measures such as rubrics. You can use a rubric to grade content, and at the same time you can use a point system for measuring specific aspects of a product. For example, a performance rubric is an excellent way to describe the content standards for an essay. But a point system may be useful for denoting the details of writing mechanics that you want students to master. Using both can give students a complete picture of your expectations, and both can easily be incorporated into your grading system.

If you choose to assign one overall grade for a project, remember to assess each separate category of a project—such as content, work ethic, collaboration, and presentation—and assign a grade for each category. This provides more explicit feedback to students on their performance on specific aspects of the project. To assign a final grade, you may decide that the weight assigned to each category differs. For example, you may decide that content is twice as important as oral presentation skills—and thus is worth twice the weight for the final grade.

Preparing a separate overall grading rubric that contains all the elements upon which the grade is based can capture this grading system. If you choose, a section called *Improvement over Time*, with appropriate indicators, can be added to a grading rubric to take account of student growth.

AVOID THE PITFALLS

Don't be overconfident in the role that Project Based Learning can play. PBL has many benefits, but one of them is not its efficiency in teaching students the basic skills of decoding, vocabulary, writing, and computation. For example, math applications can be built into projects, but math fundamentals are best taught through direct instruction.

EXAMPLES OF CULMINATING PRODUCTS

With Project Based Learning, it isn't always easy to decide what kind of culminating product you want students to produce. The following is a list of some possibilities. Most, if not all, of these products require students to have completed substantial background research. Products can be tailored to particular ages and grade levels.

- Write a proposal or create a design that proposes a solution to a difficult problem or that addresses a community issue. For example, propose a bike path or recreation area and submit the proposal to a local planning agency. The proposal might include design, environmental impact, and estimated cost.

- Study a plot of land near your school and create a plan for how that land would best be used, taking into consideration economic development, environmental concerns, recreational uses, etc.

- Research an issue of importance to your community. Propose a law that will solve a recognized problem.

- Design a model or construction that demonstrates a law, principle, or idea. Describe in writing the step-by-step process of how the construction was made, how it works, and how it demonstrates the intended concept. For example, construct a model of an atom or chemical compound, or build a model showing the process of plate tectonics and continental drift.

- Invent a device to solve a problem or to improve a process or product. Include a written explanation of the design and construction process and how the device will improve the process or product.

- Create an audio, visual, or multimedia production that conveys a particular situation or idea. Document and support your idea with written materials.

- Deliver an oral presentation of a selected topic. Document and support your presentation with written materials including sources.

- Write a magazine article about a particular topic or concept.

- Participate in a structured discussion about a specific topic or concept. Write a response that reflects on the topic, including what was learned, further questions, and connecting ideas and thoughts.

EXAMPLES OF MULTIPLE PRODUCTS

WRITTEN PRODUCTS	PRESENTATION PRODUCTS	TECHNOLOGICAL PRODUCTS	MEDIA PRODUCTS
Research report	Speech	Computer database	Audiotape
Narrative	Debate	Computer graphic	Slide show
Letter	Play	Computer program	Videotape
Poster	Song / lyric	CD-ROM	Drawing
Brief	Musical piece	Website	Painting
Proposal	Oral report		Sculpture
Poem	Panel discussion		Collage
Outline	Dramatic reenactment		Map
Brochure	Newscast		Scrapbook
Pamphlet	Discussion		Oral history
Survey / questionnaire	Dance		Photo album
Autobiography	Proposal		
Essay	Data display (e.g., chart)		
Book review	Exhibition of products		
Report			
Editorial			
Movie script			

TRAINING PRODUCTS	PLANNING PRODUCTS	CONSTRUCTION PRODUCTS
Program	Proposal	Physical model
Manual	Estimate	Consumer product
Working model	Bid	System
	Blueprint	Machine
	Flow chart	Scientific instrument
	Timeline	Museum exhibit
		Diorama

"Examples of Multiple Products" is adapted from work by John Thomas.

EXAMPLES OF ARTIFACTS

PRODUCTS THAT REVEAL PROCESS STEPS

Notes	E-mail records	Conversations	Prototypes
Journal entries	Telephone logs	Minutes of meetings	Group process reports
Descriptions of activities	Purchase receipts	Telephone bills	
Library search record	Samples	Discarded ideas	

ADVANTAGES AND DISADVANTAGES OF ASSESSMENT METHODS

Different methods of assessment have different strengths and weaknesses. You can match assessment methods to different student outcomes you have specified. The table below offers several examples.

	PRESENTATIONS	WRITTEN PRODUCTS	TESTS	SELF-REPORTS
Best Application	Content knowledge and skills.	Content knowledge, some content skills.	Content knowledge.	Habits of mind.
Advantages	Opportunities for authentic contexts. Allows students to demonstrate their work to an authentic audience. Allows for the integration of complex skills.	Allows students to work over an extended period of time and to incorporate revisions. Allows for student craftsmanship, pride, and personal embellishment.	Allows for a standardized administration to large groups of students. Useful for assessing individual students.	Allows for teacher to assess attitudes, reflections, and thinking processes of students. Allows students to identify the benefits of project work; good for identifying unanticipated consequences.
Disadvantages	Difficult to set up and administer, especially with a large number of students.	Difficult to assess individual contributions when the product is a group product. Judging what has been learned is not always evident from looking at products.	Difficult to assess skills through paper-and-pencil measures.	Difficult to establish reliable criteria.

USING BLOOM'S TAXONOMY
TO WRITE RUBRICS

LEVEL	EMPHASIS	GOAL	VERBS TO USE
1 **Knowledge**	Recognition and recall—the ability to remember facts in the way they were first presented.	Show that you know.	List, tell, define, identify, label, locate, recognize.
2 **Comprehension**	Grasp the meaning and intent of information—the ability to explain or translate into your own words.	Show that you understand.	Explain, illustrate, describe, summarize, interpret, expand, convert.
3 **Application**	Use of information—the ability to apply learning to new situations and real-life circumstances.	Show that you can use what you have learned.	Demonstrate, apply, use, construct, find solutions, collect information, perform, solve, choose appropriate procedures.
4 **Analysis**	Reasoning—the ability to break down information into component parts and to detect relationships of one part to another and to the whole.	Show that you perceive and can pick out the most important points in material presented.	Analyze, debate, differentiate, generalize, conclude, organize, determine, distinguish.
5 **Synthesis**	Originality and creativity—the ability to assemble separate parts to form a new whole.	Show that you can combine concepts to create an original or new idea.	Create, design, plan, produce, compile, develop, invent.
6 **Evaluation**	Critical assessment—the ability to use criteria or standards for evaluation and judgment.	Show that you can judge and evaluate ideas, information, procedures, and solutions.	Compare, decide, evaluate, conclude, contrast, develop criteria, assess, appraise.

AN EXAMPLE OF CATEGORIES
OF PERFORMANCE AND CRITERIA

UNDERSTANDING	WORK QUALITY	INDIVIDUAL BEHAVIOR
Demonstrates understanding	Originality	Diligence
Shows extension / application	Completeness	Timeliness
Handles questions in a way that shows mastery	Correctness	Persistence
Comprehensiveness	Appropriateness	Task focus
Adequacy of materials	Quality of arrangement or staging	Efficiency
	Quality of media use	Enthusiasm
	Quality of presentation	

A POLITICAL STUDIES PROJECT

This project has five different products.

Position Paper

CATEGORY AND WEIGHT	UNSATISFACTORY	ACCEPTABLE	ADVANCED
History of Issue 30%	Background and history of issue brief or incomplete with little or no documentation; little or no discussion of legislation or policies. Little evidence of research.	Background and history of issue adequately discussed and documented; included some dates of legislation or policies. Some evidence of research.	Background and history of issue thoroughly discussed and documented; dates of major legislation or policy decisions included. Thorough research evident.
Statement of Position 30%	Position on issue not explained or supported. Little or no evidence of critical thinking or examination of different aspects of issue.	Position on issue explained and documented.	Position on issue thoroughly explained and documented by two or more sources.
Justification or Recommendation 30%	Laws or policies on issue insufficiently justified and demonstrated, or few or no recommendations for new legislation. No research evident.	Some laws or policies on issue adequately justified and demonstrated, or some recommendations for new legislation. Limited research sources.	Laws or policies on issue clearly justified, demonstrated, and supported by multiple sources, or specific and clearly stated recommendations for new legislation.
Usage / Mechanics 10%	Basic or limited control of sentence structure with simplistic or limited word choice; a variety of repeated errors in grammar, spelling, and punctuation that cause confusion.	Adequate control of sentence structure with appropriate word choice and use of language; errors in grammar, spelling, and punctuation, but errors did not cause confusion.	Exceptional control of sentence structure with precise word choice and appropriate use of language; minimal errors in grammar, spelling, and punctuation.

Continued on next page

A POLITICAL STUDIES PROJECT, *Continued*

Political Party Web Page

CATEGORY AND WEIGHT	UNSATISFACTORY	ACCEPTABLE	ADVANCED
Form and Function 20%	Web page was poorly designed with difficult or nonfunctional navigation system or was created with little consideration of professional graphic design techniques.	The Web page had a pleasing appearance; was well organized and easy to navigate. All links worked.	The Web page was well organized and easy to navigate; was created using advanced design techniques (navigation bars, animation, color, layout, unity of font, etc.). All links worked.
Logo 5%	No logo was present or it was inappropriate.	The logo effectively represented the history or philosophy of the party.	In addition to effectively representing the history or philosophy of the party, the logo had a professional appearance.
Mission Statement / Philosophy 5%	No philosophy evident in statement.	Briefly outlined party philosophy.	Clearly outlined party philosophy and goals with specific statements about the issues most important to the party. Included statement of philosophy on the "nature of man."
Platform Issues and Positions 50%	Platform had few stated positions on major issues or positions were not fully justified and supported by research and documentation.	Platform had stated positions on all 13 required issues, including social, economic, and political topics. Some positions were fully justified and supported by research and documentation.	Platform had stated positions on at least 13 major issues, including social, economic, and political topics. All positions were fully justified and supported by research and documentation.
Grammar / Mechanics 20%	Contained significant errors that impeded understanding of content.	Contained only minor errors that did not impede understanding of content.	No errors.

Propaganda Paper

CATEGORY AND WEIGHT	UNSATISFACTORY	ACCEPTABLE	ADVANCED
Design / Appearance 50%	Poster did not appear neat or carefully designed.	Design and appearance were neat. Poster was readable.	Design was unique and creative, with much attention to detail.
Message / Content 50%	Message was unclear or diverged from positions on Web page.	Message was clear and memorable; accurately reflected positions on Web page.	Message was clear and memorable; accurately reflected positions on Web page. Content was thought-provoking.

Continued on next page

A POLITICAL STUDIES PROJECT, *Continued*

Propaganda Commercial

CATEGORY AND WEIGHT	UNSATISFACTORY	ACCEPTABLE	ADVANCED
Time Management 20%	Used significantly less than 120 seconds or was cut off.	Used slightly less than 120 seconds.	Used exactly 120 seconds.
Message / Content 40%	Message was unclear or diverged from positions on Web page.	Message was clear and memorable; accurately reflected positions on Web page.	Message was clear and memorable; accurately reflected positions on Web page. Performance was creative and entertaining.
Propaganda Techniques 20%	Did not use appeals and distraction techniques.	Used appeals and distraction techniques.	Used appeals and distraction techniques that effectively persuaded audience.
Performance 20%	Performance appeared unrehearsed.	Performers were well rehearsed and performed with few mistakes.	Performers were well rehearsed and performed without mistakes.

Campaign Speech

CATEGORY AND WEIGHT	UNSATISFACTORY	ACCEPTABLE	ADVANCED
Time Management 20% —five-minute speech —five minutes for questions	Used significantly less than five minutes for speech and did not answer questions.	Used less than five minutes for speech but filled the remainder of time by answering questions.	Used exactly five minutes for speech and answered all questions within the five-minute allotted time.
Content—Speech 40%	Message was unclear or diverged from positions on Web page. Party's position not evident from speech.	Message was clear and memorable; accurately reflected positions on Web page. Speaker was able to respond to most audience questions effectively.	Message was clear and memorable; accurately reflected positions on Web page. Speaker was able to recall information from research to support claims. Speaker was able to respond to all audience questions effectively.
Content—Questions 40%	Answers were poorly thought-out arguments and often lacked evidence or research to support party's position.	Answers were clear arguments and contained some evidence to support party's position.	Answers were clear, well thought-out arguments and contained substantial evidence to support party's position.

Note: A separate rubric was used for oral presentation skills.

"A Political Studies Project" is adapted from materials provided by Napa New Technology High School, Napa, California.

ORAL PRESENTATION I

	BEGINNING The presentation is at a beginning stage.	NOVICE The presentation may show flashes of quality, but could be improved in several important ways.	PROFICIENT The presentation is acceptable, but could be improved in a few important ways.	EXEMPLARY The presentation is exemplary.
Content	The presentation does not include information on the major points.	Important information is missing, or there are few supporting details.	Information is complete with basic supporting details, increasing audience knowledge at least to some degree.	Information is complete and well supported by detail, significantly increasing the audience's knowledge of the topic.
Thinking and Communication	The presentation does not express main points clearly, thoroughly, or persuasively.	The presentation seems to convey only limited understanding of the topic. The main points are not clearly stated or persuasive.	The presentation conveys good understanding of the topic, with some lapses. The speaker's main points are clear but are not persuasive.	The presentation conveys deep and thorough understanding of the topic. The speaker's main points are logical and persuasive.
Organization, Mechanics, and Vocabulary	No introduction is used to capture audience attention. The body of the presentation needs organization and supporting details. A suitable closing is missing. The speaker has not mastered key words and phrases relevant to the topic.	The introduction is unclear or fails to capture audience attention. The body of the presentation is confusing with limited supporting details. The closing is unclear or does not include many of the major points. The speaker's topic-related vocabulary is limited.	The introduction states the purpose but does not capture the attention of the audience. The main part of the presentation is organized and sequential with some supporting details. The closing provides a basic summary of most of the major points. Vocabulary is appropriate to the topic, with some lapses.	The introduction captures audience attention and gives a clear statement of purpose. The main part of the presentation is well organized, sequential, and well supported by detail. The closing provides a thorough summary of all of the major points. The speaker demonstrates a rich vocabulary appropriate to the topic.
Illustration	No presentation aids.	Presentation aids do not enhance audience understanding or are confusing.	Presentation aids are appropriate to the topic but are not well integrated into the overall presentation.	Presentation aids are clearly linked to the material, well executed, and informative to the audience.
Presentation	Control of speaking tone, clarity, and volume is not evident. No evidence of creativity. Speaker is visibly nervous and does not convey interest in the topic. Speaker does not make eye contact with audience. Physical gesture and awareness of facial expression are absent.	Clarity of speech is uneven; delivery is halting. Limited evidence of creativity. Speaker is not completely sure of topic; appears nervous or disengaged. Limited or sporadic eye contact with audience. Limited or inappropriate use of physical gesture and facial expression.	Good speaking voice; recovers easily from speaking errors. Creativity apparent, but it is not well integrated into presentation. Speaker is in command of the topic but appears slightly nervous in delivery. Good eye contact with audience throughout most of presentation. Use of physical gesture and facial expression is good, but appears forced or artificial at times.	Strong, clear speaking voice easily understood by audience. Use of creativity keeps audience engaged. Speaker conveys confidence in talking about the topic. Excellent eye contact with audience throughout presentation. Use of physical gesture and facial expression conveys energy and enthusiasm.

"Oral Presentation I" is adapted from Co-nect Student Project Guide, 2002.

RUBRIC EXAMPLES
ORAL PRESENTATION II

CRITERIA AND WEIGHT	UNSATISFACTORY Below performance standards	PROFICIENT Acceptable criteria	ADVANCED Demonstrates exceptional performance
Structure and Organization / 30%			*In addition to Proficient criteria:*
Introduction	No formal introduction, or introduction had no clear thesis statement. No preview of topics to be discussed.	Introduction had clear thesis statement and a preview of topics to be discussed.	Clever attention-getting introduction or an imaginative thesis and preview.
Main Ideas	Main ideas were not separated into a logical progression.	Main ideas were separated into a logical progression.	Ideas connected by original transitions, logical throughout; creative pattern.
Supporting Materials	Important ideas were not supported with references or data.	Important ideas and viewpoints were supported with accurate and detailed references to text or other works.	
Conclusion	No conclusion, or conclusion did not adequately summarize presentation.	Conclusion restated thesis statement and summarized the ideas presented.	Conclusion tied speech together, and message was memorable.
Length Requirement	Presentation did not use time allotted.	Time requirement was met for specific assignment (neither too long or too short).	Speaker used logical, ethical, and emotional appeals that enhanced a specific tone and purpose.
Vocal Expression / 20%			*In addition to Proficient criteria:*
Rate and Volume of Speech	Speaker was hard to hear or understand.	Speaker was easy to hear and understand.	Speaker was enjoyable to hear; used expression and emphasis.
Pitch, Articulation, and Pronunciation	Voice or tone distracted from purpose of presentation.	Tone was conversational, but with purpose.	Speaker used voice to create an emotional response in audience.
	Excessive use of verbal fillers.	Voice sounded natural, neither patterned nor monotone.	
		Speaker pronounced words clearly, correctly, and without verbal fillers.	
Physical Characteristics / 15%			*In addition to Proficient criteria:*
Eye Contact	Little eye contact with audience.	Strong eye contact with audience.	
Posture	Poor or slouchy posture.	Posture conveyed confidence.	Commanding, purposeful posture.
Gestures and Movement	Movements were stiff or unnatural.	Gestures and movements were natural and effective.	
Attire	Attire was inappropriate for audience.	Attire was appropriate for audience and purpose.	Attire was chosen to enhance presentation.
Appropriateness of Content and Language /15%			*In addition to Proficient criteria:*
For Audience, Purpose, and Assignment	Speaker used inappropriate language, content, or examples for this audience.	Speaker obviously considered the audience and used appropriate language and examples.	Examples and words were creative and well chosen for target audience.
	Speaker did not explain the assignment or purpose of presentation.	Speaker conveyed a clear understanding of assignment requirements and content.	
Overall Impact / 10%			*In addition to Proficient criteria:*
Energy, Enthusiasm, Sincerity, Originality / Creativity	Speaker presented the message without conviction.	Speaker appeared to believe strongly in message and demonstrated desire to have audience listen, understand, and remember.	Overall presentation was creative and exciting.
Features / 10%			*In addition to Proficient criteria:*
Multimedia, Visuals, Audio	Materials detracted from content or purpose of presentation or were of low quality.	Materials added, did not detract from presentation.	Speaker creatively integrated a variety of objects, charts, and graphs to amplify the message.
		Materials used were quality products, easy to see and hear.	

"Oral Presentation II" is adapted from materials provided by Napa New Technology High School, Napa, California, 2001–2002.

RESEARCH PAPER

| | BEGINNING | NOVICE | PROFICIENT | EXEMPLARY |
	The research paper is at a beginning stage.	The research paper may show flashes of quality, but could be improved in several ways.	The research paper is acceptable.	The research paper is exemplary.
Content	Piece is lacking information and/or information is inaccurate and irrelevant.	Provides basic information, some of which may be incorrect and/or irrelevant; based on minimal research.	Provides partially complete, accurate, and relevant information; based on adequate research.	Provides complete, accurate, and relevant information; based firmly on extensive and careful research.
Thinking and Communication	Demonstrates little understanding of the topic. Ideas are not expressed clearly or supported by examples, reasons, details, and explanations. No interpretation and analysis of the material.	Demonstrates some understanding of the topic, but with limited analysis and reflection. Ideas are not expressed clearly and examples, reasons, details, and explanations are lacking. Examines the issue from a single perspective.	Demonstrates a general understanding of the topic. Ideas are generally expressed clearly through adequate use of examples, reasons, details, or explanations. Examines the issues from more than one perspective.	Demonstrates in-depth understanding and insight into the issue(s) under discussion, through careful analysis and reflection. Ideas are developed and expressed fully and clearly, using many appropriate examples, reasons, details, or explanations. Examines the issue from three or more perspectives.
Organization, Mechanics, and Vocabulary	The written sections lack organizational devices, such as paragraphs, sections, chapters, and transitions. Numerous errors in grammar, punctuation, spelling, and/or capitalization. A bibliography or reference section is missing.	Language is copied from another source. Organizational devices, such as paragraphs, sections, chapters, and transitions, are flawed or lacking. Numerous errors in grammar, punctuation, spelling, and/or capitalization. The bibliography or reference section contains an inadequate number of primary or secondary sources.	The work is written in the author's own words. There are some problems with organizational devices, such as paragraphs, sections, chapters, and transitions. There are several errors in grammar, punctuation, spelling, and/or capitalization. A bibliography or reference section identifies an adequate number of primary and secondary sources.	All ideas are in the author's own, well-chosen words. Organizational devices, such as paragraphs, sections, chapters, and transitions, have been used effectively. With minor exceptions, grammar, punctuation, spelling, and capitalization are correct. A bibliography or reference section identifies a variety of primary and secondary sources.
Illustration	Illustrations do not help the audience understand the content and core message(s).	Visuals are unrelated or offer little support of the work. Graphics, tables, charts, diagrams, pictures, and/or models are mislabeled or irrelevant.	The work is supported by visuals. There is some mislabeling of graphics or design mistakes (e.g., a picture is confusing because it doesn't have a caption).	The work is well supported by carefully illustrated and useful tables, charts, diagrams, pictures, and/or a model—all properly labeled and captioned.
Presentation	The piece is not neat or organized, and it does not include all required elements.	The work is not neat and includes minor flaws or omissions of required elements.	The presentation is good. The overall appearance is generally neat, with a few minor flaws or missing elements.	The work is well presented and includes all required elements. The overall appearance is neat and professional.

"Research Paper" is modified from the Co-nect Student Project Guide, 2002.

CRITICAL THINKING

CRITERIA	UNSATISFACTORY Below performance standards	PROFICIENT Acceptable criteria	ADVANCED Demonstrates exceptional performance
Appropriateness The student selects material, objects, and/or techniques that meet the needs, requirements, and rules of the time, place, and audience.	Material (photos, sound files, video clips, apparel, illustrations, etc.) is not appropriate for the audience and the situation. Language is not appropriate for the audience and the situation (as defined by school and district guidelines). No evidence that student has selected an efficient tool, technique, or paradigm to achieve the goal as defined in the project or course guidelines. Humor doesn't enhance understanding and may offend audience.	Student selects material (photos, sound files, video clips, apparel, illustrations, etc.) that is appropriate for the audience and the situation. Student uses language appropriate for the audience and the situation. Student selects an effective tool, technique, or paradigm to achieve the desired goal as defined in the project or course guidelines. Student uses humor that enhances understanding and doesn't offend audience.	In addition to Proficient criteria: Student shows a deep understanding of the audience and the situation by selecting material that enhances understanding. Student uses language that creates a strong, positive reaction in audience. Student creates tools, techniques, or paradigms that effectively achieve the desired goal.
Application The student uses this material, understanding, and/or skill in new situations.	Ability to apply theories, principles, and/or skills to new situations, settings, or problems not demonstrated. Student is not able to modify theories, products, behaviors, or skills to fit new or changed environment.	Student demonstrates an ability to apply theories, principles, and/or skills to new situations, settings, or problems. Student is able to modify theories, products, behaviors, or skills to fit new or changed environment.	In addition to Proficient criteria: Student actively seeks new environments and situations to apply theories, principles, and/or skills. Student provides multiple examples of how theory, principle, or skill can be applied.
Analysis The student breaks down this material and/or skill into its component parts so that its structure can be understood.	Student does not demonstrate a clear understanding of the rules, definitions, laws, concepts, theories, and principles of topic or skill under study. Analysis does not include diagrams, models, timelines, illustrations, or step-by-step progression of object / principle / problem under study. The student does not identify cause-and-effect relationships.	Student demonstrates a clear understanding of the rules, definitions, laws, concepts, theories, and principles of topic or skill under study. Analysis includes diagrams, models, timelines, illustrations, or step-by-step progression of object / principle / problem under study. The student can identify relationships between ideas, data sets, and phenomena.	In addition to Proficient criteria: Student uses his/her analysis to teach the definitions, laws, concepts, theories, and principles under study. Student and/or audience is able to differentiate between similar definitions, laws, concepts, theories, and principles. The student can differentiate between correlation and cause and effect.
Evaluation The student judges the quality (based on both subjective and objective standards) of the material, object, or performance.	Student does not demonstrate understanding of the criteria used for evaluation. Student does not defend his/her evaluation (critique). Evaluation is not supported by reference to standards. Evaluation does not include comparison and contrast to other ideas / objects / materials.	Student demonstrates understanding of the criteria used for evaluation. Student is able to defend his/her evaluation (critique). Evaluation is supported by reference to standards. Evaluation includes comparison and contrast to other ideas / objects / materials.	In addition to Proficient criteria: Evaluation includes references (comparison / contrast) to three or more objects / ideas / materials. Student creates clearly defined criteria (e.g., rubric, standards, guidelines) for evaluation.
Synthesis The student combines more than one object or idea and forms a new, cohesive whole.	Synthesis does not successfully integrate ideas, images, and/or objects to form a cohesive whole. Student does not summarize his/her thinking during the process of synthesis. Combination of elements is not logical and/or verifiable.	Synthesis integrates ideas, images, and/or objects to form a cohesive whole. Student is able to summarize his/her thinking during the process of synthesis. Combination of elements is logical and justified.	In addition to Proficient criteria: Synthesis is unique. Synthesis shows careful planning and attention to how disparate elements fit together. Student is able to create new synthesis based on changing circumstances, input, or environment. Combination of elements is verified.

"Critical Thinking" is adapted from materials provided by Napa New Technology High School, Napa, California, 2001–2002.

PEER COLLABORATION AND TEAMWORK

CRITERIA	WEIGHT	UNSATISFACTORY	PROFICIENT	ADVANCED
Leadership and Initiative	25%	Group member played a passive role, generating few new ideas; tended to do only what they were told to do by others or did not seek help when needed.	Group member played an active role in generating new ideas, took initiative in getting tasks organized and completed, and sought help when needed.	*In addition to Proficient criteria:* The group member provided leadership to the group by thoughtfully organizing and dividing the work, checking on progress, or providing focus and direction for the project.
Facilitation and Support	25%	Group member seemed unable or unwilling to help others, made nonconstructive criticisms toward the project or other group members, or distracted other members.	Group member demonstrated willingness to help other group members when asked, actively listened to the ideas of others, and helped create a positive work environment.	*In addition to Proficient criteria:* The group member actively checked with others to understand how each member was progressing and how he or she may be of help.
Contributions and Work Ethic	50%	Group member was often off-task, did not complete assignments or duties, or had attendance problems that significantly impeded progress on project. May have worked hard, but on relatively unimportant parts of the project.	Group member was prepared to work each day, met due dates by completing assignments / duties, and worked hard on the project most of the time. If absent, other group members knew the reason, and progress was not significantly impeded.	*In addition to Proficient criteria:* The group member made up for work left undone by other group members and demonstrated willingness to spend significant time outside of class / school to complete the project.

"Peer Collaboration and Teamwork" is adapted from materials provided by Napa New Technology High School, Napa, California, 2001–2002.

CREATING A RUBRIC FOR ACCESSING INFORMATION

1. Use the following elements for an *Accessing Information* rubric:

	LIMITED	DEVELOPING	PROFICIENT	ADVANCED	EXEMPLARY
Displays a strategic approach when accessing information.					
Accesses a variety of information sources.					
Searches for a variety of perspectives.					
Uses information retrieval systems and technology.					
Asks appropriate questions about information access.					
Seeks assistance when needed.					

2. Add descriptors depicting what students do as they develop the information access expertise needed to complete the project. Here is an example of criteria for the first element of the rubric:

	LIMITED	DEVELOPING	PROFICIENT	ADVANCED	EXEMPLARY
Displays a strategic approach when accessing information.	Searches for information randomly or without an explicit search strategy.		Provides evidence of a strategic approach and describes explicit plan.		Can explain and demonstrate an explicit and comprehensive search strategy appropriate for the question being addressed.

"Creating a Rubric for Accessing Information" is adapted from materials provided by Sir Francis Drake High School, San Anselmo, California, and Tamalpais Union High School District, Larkspur, California.

CREATING A RUBRIC FOR SELECTING INFORMATION

1. Use the following elements for a *Selecting Information* rubric:

	LIMITED	DEVELOPING	PROFICIENT	ADVANCED	EXEMPLARY
Searches key sources efficiently.					
Focuses on key sources.					
Selects key ideas from sources.					
Records information efficiently.					
Organizes and labels selected information.					
Clarifies information as needed.					

2. Add descriptors depicting what students do as they develop the information selection expertise needed to complete the project. Here is an example of criteria for the first element of the rubric:

	LIMITED	DEVELOPING	PROFICIENT	ADVANCED	EXEMPLARY
Searches key sources efficiently.	Does not focus on key sources, or is not selective in finding information.		Obtains relevant information from key sources and makes effective use of skimming strategies.		Obtains relevant and wide-ranging information from key sources quickly using skimming and search strategies (index, key words).

"Creating a Rubric for Selecting Information" is adapted from materials provided by Sir Francis Drake High School, San Anselmo, California, and Tamalpais Union High School District, Larkspur, California.

CREATING A RUBRIC FOR PROCESSING INFORMATION

1. Use the following elements for a *Processing Information* rubric:

	LIMITED	DEVELOPING	PROFICIENT	ADVANCED	EXEMPLARY
Draws connections between ideas.					
Identifies and labels key information and ideas.					
Organizes data and ideas.					
Labels and categorizes notes.					
Interprets information.					
Summarizes information.					

2. Add descriptors depicting what students do as they develop the information processing expertise needed to complete the project. Here is an example of criteria for the first element of the rubric:

	LIMITED	DEVELOPING	PROFICIENT	ADVANCED	EXEMPLARY
Draws connections between ideas.	Reads and records verbatim information. Does not comment on connections among ideas.		Notes and summaries show interconnections between ideas within a single source.		Notes and summaries contain insightful comments on the relationship between ideas across multiple sources.

"Creating a Rubric for Processing Information" is adapted from materials provided by Sir Francis Drake High School, San Anselmo, California, and Tamalpais Union High School District, Larkspur, California.

CREATING A RUBRIC FOR COMPOSING A PRESENTATION

1. Use the following elements for a *Composing a Presentation* rubric:

	LIMITED	DEVELOPING	PROFICIENT	ADVANCED	EXEMPLARY
Creates a convincing, authoritative argument.					
Exhibits creativity in composition.					
Puts information in own words.					
Develops main ideas and organizing concepts.					
Provides sufficient evidence to support claims.					
Provides examples and concrete details.					

2. Add descriptors depicting what students do as they develop the presentation expertise needed to complete the project. Here is an example of criteria for the first element of the rubric:

	LIMITED	DEVELOPING	PROFICIENT	ADVANCED	EXEMPLARY
Creates a convincing, authoritative argument.	Provides inconsistent evidence for position.		Argues a position based on sufficient evidence.		Builds a logical, step-by-step case using a variety of information and persuasive evidence.

"Creating a Rubric for Composing a Presentation" is adapted from materials provided by Sir Francis Drake High School, San Anselmo, California, and Tamalpais Union High School District, Larkspur, California.

CREATING A RUBRIC FOR MAKING A PRESENTATION

1. Use the following elements for a *Making a Presentation* rubric:

	LIMITED	DEVELOPING	PROFICIENT	ADVANCED	EXEMPLARY
Uses visuals clearly and effectively.					
Communicates and stresses main points.					
Body posture projects confidence and authority.					
Makes consistent eye contact.					
Enunciates clearly with appropriate volume.					
Makes minimal pauses and avoids filler words.					

2. Add descriptors depicting what students do as they develop the presentation expertise needed to complete the project. Here is an example of criteria for the first element of the rubric:

	LIMITED	DEVELOPING	PROFICIENT	ADVANCED	EXEMPLARY
Uses visuals clearly and effectively.	Visuals not tightly linked to presentation; do not support or clarify main points.		Visuals clarify and illustrate main points.		Highly developed, memorable visuals clarify and illustrate main points; presenter integrates and manages visuals skillfully.

"Creating a Rubric for Making a Presentation" is adapted from materials provided by Sir Francis Drake High School, San Anselmo, California, and Tamalpais Union High School District, Larkspur, California.

CREATING A RUBRIC FOR INDIVIDUAL TASK MANAGEMENT

1. Use the following elements for an *Individual Task Management* rubric:

	LIMITED	DEVELOPING	PROFICIENT	ADVANCED	EXEMPLARY
Solicits and uses feedback.					
Sets appropriate and realistic goals.					
Works independently with minimal supervision.					
Perseveres appropriately.					
Carries out tasks carefully and diligently.					
Meets deadlines.					

2. Add descriptors depicting what students do as they develop the task management expertise needed to complete the project. Here is an example of criteria for the first element of the rubric:

	LIMITED	DEVELOPING	PROFICIENT	ADVANCED	EXEMPLARY
Solicits and uses feedback.	Does not see the need for feedback; does not solicit or use feedback.		Uses feedback to improve performance.		Seeks out feedback and uses information to improve products or performance.

"Creating a Rubric for Individual Task Management" is adapted from materials provided by Sir Francis Drake High School, San Anselmo, California, and Tamalpais Union High School District, Larkspur, California.

CREATING A RUBRIC FOR INDIVIDUAL TIME MANAGEMENT

1. Use the following elements for an *Individual Time Management* rubric:

	LIMITED	DEVELOPING	PROFICIENT	ADVANCED	EXEMPLARY
Uses time effectively.					
Estimates time realistically.					
Establishes a schedule for completing work.					
Allocates time among tasks strategically.					
Stays on schedule.					
Completes tasks on a timely basis.					

2. Add descriptors depicting what students do as they develop the time management expertise needed to complete the project. Here is an example of criteria for the first element of the rubric:

	LIMITED	DEVELOPING	PROFICIENT	ADVANCED	EXEMPLARY
Uses time effectively.	Does not recognize the reality of time constraints or take actions to use available time efficiently.		Uses time efficiently and completes work within given time constraints.		Prioritizes tasks, recognizes time constraints, estimates time to completion, and avoids distraction while meeting deadlines and using time effectively.

"Creating a Rubric for Individual Time Management" is adapted from materials provided by Sir Francis Drake High School, San Anselmo, California, and Tamalpais Union High School District, Larkspur, California.

CREATING A RUBRIC FOR GROUP TASK AND TIME MANAGEMENT

1. Use the following elements for a *Group Task and Time Management* rubric:

	LIMITED	DEVELOPING	PROFICIENT	ADVANCED	EXEMPLARY
Monitors group progress.					
Sets appropriate and realistic goals.					
Develops a plan for completing group work.					
Keeps track of materials.					
Maintains group focus on what's important.					
Allocates time effectively.					

2. Add descriptors depicting what students do as they develop the group task and time management expertise needed to complete the project. Here is an example of criteria for the first element of the rubric:

	LIMITED	DEVELOPING	PROFICIENT	ADVANCED	EXEMPLARY
Monitors progress.	Group does not attempt to monitor its progress or fails to do so when requested.		Group monitors and assesses progress as necessary.		Group regularly monitors and assesses progress of individual members and group as a whole using structured discussion.

"Creating a Rubric for Group Task and Time Management" is adapted from materials provided by Sir Francis Drake High School, San Anselmo, California, Tamalpais Union High School District, Larkspur, California, and Northwest Regional Educational Laboratory, Portland, Oregon.

CREATING A RUBRIC FOR GROUP PROCESS

1. Use the following elements for a *Group Process* rubric:

	LIMITED	DEVELOPING	PROFICIENT	ADVANCED	EXEMPLARY
Group members facilitate each other's participation.					
All group members participate in project work.					
Work is distributed and completed.					
Group coordinates well with other groups.					
Group uses members' strengths effectively.					
Group members resolve conflicts successfully.					

2. Add descriptors depicting what students do as they develop the group process expertise needed to complete the project. Here is an example of criteria for the first element of the rubric:

	LIMITED	DEVELOPING	PROFICIENT	ADVANCED	EXEMPLARY
Group members facilitate each other's participation.	Members show little interest in the contributions of others and interrupt frequently.		Members encourage everyone to contribute fully.		Members often encourage other members to share thinking, listen carefully, and effectively manage disruptive behavior.

"Creating a Rubric for Group Process" is adapted from materials provided by Sir Francis Drake High School, San Anselmo, California, Tamalpais Union High School District, Larkspur, California, and Northwest Regional Educational Laboratory, Portland, Oregon.

PROJECT GRADING WORKSHEET

Total Possible Project Points from All Assessments [ ]

	ASSESSMENT	DATE	PERCENT OF GRADE	POINTS POSSIBLE	POINTS EARNED
Teacher Observation	Observation #1				
	Observation #2				
	Observation #3				
Tests	Test #1				
	Test #2				
	Test #3				
Products	Product #1				
	Product #2				
	Product #3				
Student Self-Assessment	Self-Assessment #1				
	Self-Assessment #2				
	Self-Assessment #3				
Performances	Performance #1				
	Performance #2				
	Performance #3				
Other					

BLANK RUBRIC
Rubric Title

CRITERIA	LIMITED	DEVELOPING	PROFICIENT	ADVANCED	EXEMPLARY

BEGIN WITH THE END IN MIND

Designing and Planning Successful Projects

CRAFT THE DRIVING QUESTION

PLAN THE ASSESSMENT

MAP THE PROJECT

MANAGE THE PROCESS

Contents

IDEA BANK

Analyzing instructional needs, planning activities, estimating time, and preparing resources are key tasks in a project. This section highlights these tasks—and shows you how to be successful as a project planner.

MAP THE PROJECT

Constructing a lesson plan is a familiar exercise for teachers. A project map is similar to a lesson plan, but it reflects the extended nature of projects and the need to *structure* the project. A well-constructed project map includes more than a sequence of activities; it is a design for supporting and directing students as they create products in the project. A map helps you identify the requisite skills that your students need to perform, develop the timeline for the project, and gather resources to support critical learning activities in the project.

KEY STEPS

1 Organize Tasks and Activities

Breaking down the products in the project into a set of tasks is not only essential for solid assessment planning, but it also helps you allocate the right amount of time for each task. How detailed you wish to be in analyzing the tasks in a project is up to you, but it is helpful to write out the tasks with enough specifics for you to identify any resources you may have to gather for students.

Prior to a project, analyze the products required, and then take a close look at your students. Do they know enough to succeed at the tasks in the project? For example, does the project include an exhibition and an oral presentation—have students been taught and practiced oral presentations? Do they know how to do an interview? Research on the Web? Until you can answer questions like this affirmatively, you may not want to begin the actual project. Instead, spend time preparing students by having them first practice crucial project skills or learning essential information. In the end, that will save you time and increase the chances for a successful project.

Scaffolding is the educational term for building the knowledge and skills that students need to take on a new task. Note that this is not an argument for putting off a project until the end of the school year. Projects *pull* students through a difficult curriculum, and sometimes it's best to have them learn through that process rather than be taught through direct instruction.

The following is an example that uses a section from the BIE Project Planning forms to illustrate how one product—a mock Business

Plan—might be broken down into a series of tasks in a "Start Your Own Business" project. The chart includes the knowledge and skills that need to be taught prior to the project.

Project Planning Form

Look at one major product for the project, and analyze the tasks necessary to produce a high-quality product. What do students need to know and be able to do to complete the tasks successfully? How and when will they learn the necessary knowledge and skills? Complete for all major products for the project.

Product: MOCK BUSINESS PLAN

KNOWLEDGE AND SKILLS NEEDED	ALREADY HAVE LEARNED	TAUGHT BEFORE THE PROJECT	TAUGHT DURING THE PROJECT
1. Know Business Plan format			✓
2. Interview skills		✓	
3. Editing	✓		
4. Know Excel		✓	
5. Know how to project a budget			✓
6. Calculating profit and loss			✓
7. Calculating interest on loans			✓

2 Decide How to Launch the Project

In Project Based Learning, projects begin in many different ways. A class discussion, a field trip, an article, a guest lecturer, an activity —all these can be used to provoke thinking and engage students in the project. They can be considered as *entry events* for a project.

Problem-based projects often employ an *entry document*. An entry document is designed as a scenario-builder that outlines the problem or issue, defines the students' roles and tasks, and sets forth the expectations for successful work in the project. A thought-provoking beginning to a project generates enthusiasm and interest. In the **Idea Bank** for this section, you will find a sample entry document from the BIE Problem Based Economics materials that illustrates how the document can be written.

Whether you use an entry event or entry document to launch the project, the essential goal is to begin helping students quickly to understand the scope of the project, the products that will be required, and the assessments that will take place in the project.

3 Gather Resources

Teachers are experts at gathering resources. But projects are time-consuming and require a great deal of constant conversation with students. It is wise to plan ahead by preparing a list of Websites to research, copying project forms, calling to reserve the computer lab, recruiting a group of adults to attend the final exhibition, or carrying out the many other tasks necessary for successful project management. A resource list is included in the **Idea Bank**.

Resources include information (books, people, Internet sites), supplies necessary to complete project products (notebooks, construction paper, display boards), and technological tools (computers, cameras, printers) useful for completing project tasks. Resources might be items that are already available and can be incorporated into the project, as well as items that must be located, collected, ordered, or purchased.

Some tips on resources:

- **Resources almost always require some preparation or training.** Allocating time within project activities for students to learn to use the resources productively is an essential part of project planning.

AVOID THE PITFALLS

Don't rely on technology because it's available or fun. Technological tools can supplement PBL, but they should rarely be the central focus of the project. Use technology as a tool for learning.

Be wary of dividing student labor. When there are central ideas that everyone should understand, or critical skills that everyone should obtain, division of labor can lead to differential learning and differential commitment to the task. Structure group work so that all students learn common core concepts.

Don't let the activity drive the instructional content. Let the instructional content drive the activity. It can be compelling to have an interesting activity idea and then try to "shoehorn" in content from the curriculum. However, it is far better to start with the content, i.e., powerful, central ideas or complex concepts, then plan activities around this content in such a way that the challenge associated with the project is in discovering and using subject-matter principles.

- **Technological resources can be a double-edged sword.** They can significantly expand the power of the project in many ways and contribute to students' motivation to participate. At the same time, technological resources can delay project progress, overwhelm teachers and students alike, distract students from the central content to be learned, or shift the project emphasis from learning content to managing technology. Emphasizing technology in place of content can take up time, encourage "splash" at the expense of deep learning, and mask the fact that students have not done sufficient work to solve the problem or address the issues raised by the Driving Question.

- **Resources should be selected in order to increase the power of the project.** Although students often enjoy using resources —especially technological resources—not all resources foster student learning. Resources are most powerful in supporting project work when they increase the efficiency of project tasks, increase the information available to students, or allow students to investigate critical concepts or principles more thoroughly, more meaningfully, or more realistically.

4 Draw a "Storyboard"

Once you have outlined the main activities for the project, sketch out the project in a visual format such as a bubble diagram, flow chart, or storyboard format. Create a timeline for the project and identify major milestones and assignments, along with other important activities such as the following:

The project launch	Due dates for drafts or
Sequence of activities	rehearsals
Preparation of drafts,	Due dates for products
rehearsals, practices,	Exams
prototypes, etc.	Homework assignments
Scaffold lessons	Reflection and review

On the next page is an example of a storyboard for a four-week, 7th-grade English, United States history, and multimedia project titled *Getting Away with Murder.*

Map the Project

Draw a storyboard for this project. Include a timeline, major activities, and important milestones.

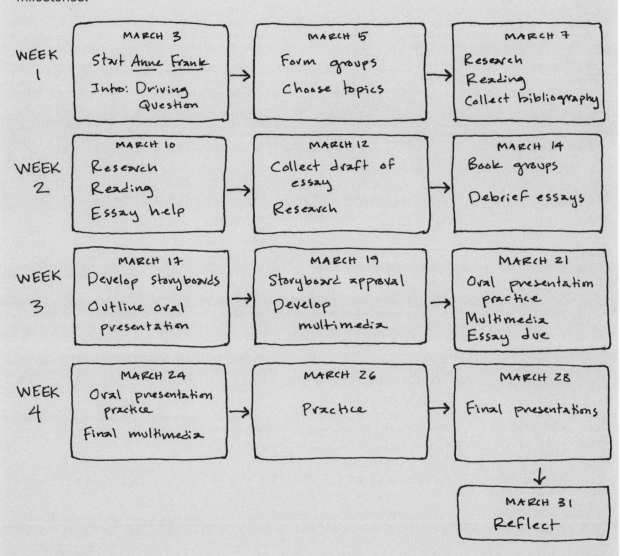

WEEK 1

MARCH 3
Start Anne Frank
Intro: Driving Question

→ MARCH 5
Form groups
Choose topics

→ MARCH 7
Research
Reading
Collect bibliography

WEEK 2

MARCH 10
Research
Reading
Essay help

→ MARCH 12
Collect draft of essay
Research

→ MARCH 14
Book groups
Debrief essays

WEEK 3

MARCH 17
Develop storyboards
Outline oral presentation

→ MARCH 19
Storyboard approval
Develop multimedia

→ MARCH 21
Oral presentation practice
Multimedia
Essay due

WEEK 4

MARCH 24
Oral presentation practice
Final multimedia

→ MARCH 26
Practice

→ MARCH 28
Final presentations

↓ MARCH 31
Reflect

List resources you will need for the project:

Computer Lab   March 17-24

Multipurpose Room   March 28

PROJECT ACTIVITIES AND TASKS

Activities need to be broken down into a series of tasks. Here are ideas on how major activities in your project can be organized by tasks.

PLANNING

Develop task charts, timelines, flow charts
Create a concept map
Develop a blueprint
Develop a design brief

BREAKING THE PROBLEM INTO PARTS

Develop a taxonomy
Develop a formal model
Shadow an expert

EXPANDING KNOWLEDGE

Conduct formal interviews
Hold a panel discussion or debate
Engage in Socratic dialogue
Develop / administer questionnaires
Listen to experts
Apprentice or intern
Conduct a focus group
Conduct a case study
Compose a theory
Brainstorm
Seek solutions by using analogies
Look for solutions by examining similar problems

COORDINATING

Settle a dispute between people or groups
Conduct a meeting using formal rules of order
Institute "idea bins," "in boxes," "to-do lists"
Institute "jigsaw" methods for collaborative learning
Create a database to organize information

ASSESSMENTS

Build rubrics
Conduct a cost-benefit analysis
Critique a product according to real-world standards
Use criteria to rate proposals, products, or ideas

COMMUNICATING

Defend a position
Present
Report on an event
Teach a skill to a novice
Create diagrams
Modify a presentation for other audiences

Examples on pages 88–90 are adapted from the work of John Thomas.

EXAMPLES OF PROJECT ACTIVITIES

DESCRIPTIVE RESEARCH

Location of information
- Observation excursions
- Surveying experts

Collection and organization of information
- Observing
- Reading and noting
- Surveying
- Interviewing
- E-mail queries of experts
- Categorization of information
- Organized information collages
- Factstorming (e.g., using a large board or wall to record information generated)
- Sorting and labeling—looking for similarities and differences; looking for overarching categories

Synthesizing information
- Drafting paragraphs that relate information (notes on notes)
- Drawing or graphing new ideas
- Sequencing information
- Drafting introductions and conclusions
- Organizing the parts into a cohesive report
- Collection, organization, and evaluation of information
- Interpreting written works
- Evaluating the work of others

HYPOTHESIS TESTING

Data collection
Generating hypotheses
Experimentation—controlling variables
Experimentation—product test
Experimentation—comparison of products or processes

ANALYSIS

Analyzing perspectives—panel discussions, seminars, debates
Error analysis
Operational analysis
- Finding out how something works
- Increasing the efficiency of a process

Structural analysis
- Investigating how a structure works

Semantic feature analysis
- Mapping, e.g., words, concepts, central ideas

Cost-benefit analysis
Comparing / Classifying

DESIGN

Spatial problem solving
Mapping
Building a model
Building a simulation
Designing a product to meet specifications
Designing a process to meet specifications
Product improvement
Process improvement

COMPOSITION

Notetaking / Notemaking
Synthesizing categorized information into a new scheme
Composing outlines
Drafting cohesive paragraphs based on syntheses of information
Sequencing paragraphs and ideas
Drafting introductions and conclusions

DIAGNOSES

Solving mysteries
Finding causes, e.g., medical detection or clinical diagnoses

CONDUCTING PROBLEM-SOLVING EPISODES

Interpreting clues
Identifying problems
Defining problems
Seeking solutions
Generating ideas
Trying out solutions
Evaluating solutions

DECISION MAKING

Applying decision-making strategies
Generating decision criteria
Resolving disputes, negotiating, compromising
Testing solution ideas
Solving moral dilemmas, relational problems

MODEL-BUILDING RESEARCH

Reconstruction of events—role-playing, reenactment
Explanation building, theory building
Pattern building, e.g., through observation
Meaning making, e.g., clinical, legal, literary, historical case studies

SCAFFOLDING IDEAS

Ways to Provide Scaffolding

DIRECT INSTRUCTION

Lectures, presentations
Films with discussions
Training sessions
Reading assignments with follow-up

HANDOUTS AND FORMS

Checklists
Templates
Timelines
Rubrics
Charts
Skeletons
Outlines
Models

ORIENTATIONS

Cues, labels, signs
List of steps, rules, roles
Written examples, samples
Oral instructions
Advance organizers
Rules of order
Graphic organizers

GUIDED PRACTICE

Rehearsals
Pilot tests
Apprenticeships
Tutorials
Training sessions
Imaging
Modeling

FEEDBACK EVENTS

Apprenticeships
Tutorials
Reflection opportunities
Peer review
Simulated tryouts
Debriefings

SELF-MANAGEMENT TRAINING

Self-monitoring, reflection
Planning
Goal setting
Self-direction, self-cueing
Self-reinforcement
Self-assessment

Scaffolding to Build Skills

GROUP PROCESS

Rules of order
Role descriptions
Guidance in listening skills
Decision-making steps
Problem-solving
  framework

TECHNOLOGY

Tutorial audio and video
  tapes
"How-to" books
Overheads

TIME MANAGEMENT

Contracting
Estimating and recording
  time allocations
Wall "progress" charts
Wall calendar
"Time In" and "Time Out"
  books

PROBLEM SOLVING

Idea generation techniques
  (e.g., rules of
  brainstorming)
Pre-printed forms with
  steps and hints

DECISION MAKING

Training in the use of
  decision-making
  models
Checklists

RESEARCH

Training in specific
  research techniques
Pre-printed data forms with
  strategies and
  questions indicated

COMMUNICATION SKILLS

Films on how to conduct a
  telephone survey
Role-playing exercises
Telephone scripts

TECHNICAL WRITING

Skeleton forms to guide
  descriptive writing
Cue cards
Half-finished examples

PERSUASIVE WRITING

Advance organizers
Outlines
Cue cards
Say it, then write it

COMPLEX OPERATIONS

Reciprocal teaching (taking
  turns playing the roles
  of teacher and giving
  guidance and
  feedback)

SELF-EVALUATION

Models of other students'
  evaluation forms
Checklists

METACOGNITION

Coached apprenticeship
Testifying in group settings
Telling without showing

IDEA BANK IDEA BANK IDEA BA

SAMPLE ENTRY DOCUMENT

Oak Grove City High School
Home of the Wildcats
Dr. Stanley Campbell, Principal

TO: Student Council, Oak Grove City High School
via Bart Stravinsky, Student Council President
FROM: Dr. Stanley Campbell, Principal, Oak Grove City High School
REGARDING: Food Court in the New Student Center

As you know, the School Board unanimously voted last night to allow the Student Council to select the restaurants for the Food Court that will be housed in our new student center. We advertised widely throughout the city inviting restaurants to apply for a space in the Food Court. Twelve restaurants have applied for space. Unfortunately, we have space for only five restaurants. The School Board has set the following parameters to help you make your decision as to which five restaurants should be allowed space in the Food Court.

1) Restaurants will share a percentage of their profits from food sold at the Food Court with the Student Council. The Student Council will be allowed to spend this money in any way they see fit subject to the guidelines set by the Student Council by-laws. Since this revenue is the only money the Student Council has in its budget, your first task might be to determine which restaurants will yield the most profit. The more revenue you generate from the Food Court, the more clubs, student activities, and social events you can afford to fund.

2) Each of the twelve restaurants has agreed to pay the Student Council 20 percent of its profits for space in the Food Court. Should the restaurant not make a profit, no money will be paid to the Student Council. The less money paid to the Student Council, the more you will have to cancel, or charge fees for, events you sponsor.

3) There will be no set-up fees for the restaurants, and each restaurant requires the same space allocation.

4) You are free to use whatever criteria you wish to select the five restaurants that will ultimately operate in our Food Court. However, keep in mind that you are, as members of the Student Council, representatives of all the interests in the school. You need to take into account the needs of all the students when making your restaurant selections. This is particularly important since we have a closed campus and students must buy their lunch at our Food Court.

5) The President of our Board is an economist. So, remember that regardless of your decision, the rationale must be grounded in sound economic thinking.

6) Your selection will be in effect for four years as each restaurant you choose will be given a four-year contract.

7) You must justify your selections to the School Board at its meeting in one week.

8) The School Board will vote on whether to approve your recommendation. They must reach a consensus on your recommendation, which means that the Board members must all agree that the plan is acceptable. Their vote will be based upon how compelling your presentation is. You must be able to justify your choice of restaurants based upon whether they meet the needs of students and are profitable. If the School Board does not accept your proposal and its justification, they will ask you to return the following week with a revised proposal. Your visual presentation, with posters and graphs, must be given to the Board's secretary two days before the meeting for its inclusion in the meeting agenda.

PROJECT RESOURCES FORM

PROJECT: **STUDENT(S):**   **DATE:**

Websites

Books / Other Sources

Instructional Materials

Other Technology

Parent and Community Volunteers

Continued on next page

Mentors

Organizations / Programs / Places

People

Consultants / Experts

Business and Community Groups

BEGIN WITH THE END IN MIND

Designing and Planning Successful Projects

CRAFT THE DRIVING QUESTION

PLAN THE ASSESSMENT

MAP THE PROJECT

MANAGE THE PROCESS

Contents

MANAGE THE PROCESS

As a PBL teacher, you can successfully manage the process of learning by using tools and strategies that bring structure and accountability to the process. This section offers specific recommendations for managing and evaluating a project.

Experience with projects is necessary to master the skills of project leadership. In this section guidelines for successful project management are accompanied by forms in the **Idea Bank** that provide specific aid for grouping and managing students. The next section, **What Do PBL Teachers Say?**, contains practical advice on managing projects.

ANTICIPATING YOUR ROLE

Anticipating the various roles you will play as a project manager is important. If you are working as a member of a project team, you should discuss these roles and tasks with colleagues. Also, discussing your responsibilities with students at the beginning of the project helps clarify what is expected of the teacher and students in the project.

What will you have to do to manage a successful project? Here is a list of critical management tasks:

- **Orient** students to the goals of the project, not only at the beginning, but also on a regular basis as the project progresses. Continuously reinforce the goals of the project, often by referring to the Driving Question, to keep students focused and motivated. On longer projects, remind students regularly of their progress. Communicate next steps to help students stay on task, and remind them that in-depth learning takes time and patience.

- **Group** students appropriately. Collaboration is a hallmark of PBL, but collaboration takes place in different ways. Students may work in small groups or as a whole group. They may work individually on products and collaborate only on rubrics or presentations. Also, the groupings may change as the project progresses. Choosing the appropriate grouping mode is part of project planning and management. See the **Idea Bank** for useful ideas on grouping.

- **Organize** the project on a daily basis by continually defining the scope of inquiry, the study tasks, and the potential routes to solving the problem or answering the Driving Question. You are responsible for setting and enforcing deadlines, collecting artifacts from students as the project progresses, and offering the feedback that is necessary for keeping students on track toward successful completion of the project.

- **Clarify** everything. Projects involve multitasking and decision making, with students making choices about where they should put their time and energy. Students will have many questions about what to do next or what is important to know. Be prepared to direct their efforts clearly.

- **Monitor and regulate** student behavior. Projects require students to move about the classroom, work independently, and sometimes leave the school campus to conduct research. This makes it necessary for teachers to train students in how to work effectively with less supervision, especially if students are accustomed to a more passive role in the classroom. Students need time limits, benchmarks, directions for managing time, scheduling aids such as daily goal sheets, and deadlines to learn to manage independent time. Similarly, you may have to regulate their use of resources and supplies during projects, until students are able to manage on their own.

- **Manage** the workflow. This requires the usual collection of homework or other assignments at the right time. It also requires a constant watch on how the project is progressing and whether students are on track to complete the project successfully. Watch for content areas in which students feel deficient or for tasks that prove too easy or too hard for a majority of students. If necessary, stop and use "just-in-time" instruction—a quick lecture, handout, or other conventional source of information to give students the content they need to proceed.

- **Evaluate** the success of the project and help students recognize what has been learned—and what has not been learned—as a result of the project.

KEY STEPS

1 Share Project Goals with Students

Students and teachers working together can create many successful projects. But you may prefer to develop and present the project to your students. If so, one of the most effective strategies you can use is to share the goals and context for the project with your students as early as possible. Research on goals shows that young people do not have to create the project in order to feel motivated and perform well. However, goals are more likely to be met if they are relevant and important to students' lives. If you have planned and outlined a worthy project, share your vision with students. Let them know how the project can benefit themselves, their school, or their community. Taking special care to connect the goals of the project to the futures of the students will go a long way toward starting off a project in the most successful way possible.

Refining Projects with Students

You may have a well-planned project, but students may be able to improve the plan or shape it toward their particular interests. This can be done through whole-class discussion or through a structured activity that teaches them vital listening and planning skills. One method is the Tuning Protocol, or Critical Friends Protocol, which is a structured method for discussing plans for a project at the outset or for presenting findings as the project progresses. The protocol uses small groups to discuss projects and receive feedback. Two or three small groups (four to five students each) may be placed together in a Tuning Protocol. See the **Idea Bank** for instructions on this method.

2 Use Problem-Solving Tools

Part of the management plan for the project is choosing tools that will assist students in focusing on the problem or issue and tracking their thinking as they progress toward solutions and explanations. The following list includes three key tools useful in both project and problem based learning:

- **A know / need-to-know list** is an excellent tool for helping students to understand the parameters of a problem or project at the beginning. Using two flip charts or two columns on a single flip chart, students as a group list everything that they know about the problem or the Driving Question. The list is inclusive rather than exclusive. That is, students should be encouraged to list all the observations they can make about the topic, even if some of the observations appear obvious. Similarly, students then create a list of everything they need to know to solve the problem or answer the question. The result is two lists—one that demonstrates what students know and understand, and one that contains a list of investigations that must take place. As the investigations are completed and reveal more information about the problem, both lists change as items are added or crossed off.

- **Learning logs** contain daily or other journal entries by students describing the progress of their investigations. Learning logs are useful for documenting the "how" of a project, including the frustrations and breakthroughs of the problem-solving process. Learning logs can be graded and are an excellent way to create an artifact that documents the process of PBL.
- **Planning, investigation, and product briefs** focus student attention on the problem and encourage students to be persistent in their research. They are also a useful class management tool. Samples are included in the **Idea Bank** for this section.

3 Use Checkpoints and Milestones

A formal or informal system is necessary to monitor student learning as the project progresses. Using a management system provides a means for breaking the project into separate components that allow for revisions "on the fly," ensuring that the project outcomes will be met. A number of useful methods exist to accomplish this. Most involve the use of artifacts that provide a record of the progress of a project, such as:

- Ask group leaders to give informal briefings on group progress
- Assign quick writes to groups or to the entire class
- Interview random or selected students
- Survey individuals and groups
- Schedule weekly reflection sessions for groups and/or the whole class
- Review student or class checklists of completed project steps
- Examine progress logs completed by individual students or groups
- Write your own project journal
- "Sit in" with groups to monitor progress
- Conduct debriefing sessions following activity or product completion

Project progress can be focused on various aspects of the project, including:

- Problems in understanding how to carry out project activities
- Progress / benchmark accomplishments of students and groups

- Motivation / participation of individual students and groups
- Problems / successes with particular activities or products
- Unexpected accomplishments
- New strategies devised by individual students and groups
- Student needs for specific resources or instructional support

4 Plan for Evaluation and Reflection

Students who have the opportunity to discuss, analyze, and reflect on their learning experiences are more likely to retain and use their knowledge and skills. Scheduling sufficient time at the end of the project for a class "debriefing" to analyze the results of the project helps students take what they have learned and transfer it to the next project or assignment. In particular, it is useful to have students reflect on and discuss the Driving Question again. The **Idea Bank** following this section provides evaluation and reflection forms that students can use to help them conserve what they have learned.

> Students who have the opportunity to discuss, analyze, and reflect on their learning experiences are more likely to retain and use their knowledge and skills.

The Culminating Evaluation

A culminating evaluation also encourages the habits and skills of reflection and analysis—a lifelong learning skill and an essential skill in today's workplace. The questions or the topics for discussion can be focused on content, but also on the process and outcomes for the project. For example:

- What did we learn?
- Did we collaborate effectively?
- What skills did we learn?
- What skills do we need to practice?
- What was the quality of our work?
- Where can we improve?

A culminating evaluation of the project can be done individually or collaboratively. However the evaluation is done, the results should be shared with students. To reinforce the learning, capture student comments and evaluations on a flip chart or on a whiteboard, and keep the information visible for a week or so. Here are four methods that work well for a culminating evaluation:

- **Whole-class debriefing session.** This method underscores the importance of reflection to students and builds a sense of common standards and learning goals in the classroom. Using a student facilitator, along with a set of questions to guide the discussion, reinforces the skills of active listening, collaboration, presentation, and critical assessment.
- **Fishbowl.** A variation of the whole-class discussion is to have small groups of students debrief in the center of the classroom, with the remainder of the class acting as an audience but also able to occasionally participate in the discussion. See the **Idea Bank** for instructions on this method.
- **Survey.** Simple surveys can be constructed to give students the opportunity to comment on the project. As with all surveys, the results are more powerful if shared and interpreted with the respondents.
- **Self-evaluation.** This applies to students and teachers. Teachers may want to reflect formally on the process and results of the project. Students should also have the opportunity to reflect on their individual learning and progress. The **Idea Bank** contains samples of forms for this purpose.

Celebration

In addition to evaluating and reflecting at the end of a project, remember to celebrate. When students have invested their time and energy in a successful project, especially a major project, help them acknowledge what they have accomplished. Include parents, community members, other teachers, or anyone else who was involved in the project. The celebration can be part of the debriefing day, or planned as a special event such as a reception, ceremony, or presentation of awards.

SAMPLE LETTER
TO PARENTS

Date

Dear Parents,

I am writing to tell you about an innovative learning experience we are about to undertake in *(name of teacher, period, and class)*. Your son or daughter will be participating in a project entitled *(name of project)*. We will be working on this project for approximately *(duration)* weeks.

The purpose of this project is to *(project purpose)*. Your student will be involved in the following activities *(researching in the library, interviewing community members, preparing an oral presentation, using the Web to communicate with students in other countries, etc.)*.

At the conclusion of the *(name of project)*, students will present to the public what they have learned. This presentation will take place in the *(location)* and is scheduled for *(date)* at *(time)*. We hope you will be able to attend.

Project work requires more resources than traditional teaching. It would be a great help if parents could contribute the following items *(art supplies, city maps, refreshments, expertise, etc.)*.

Please contact me if you have any questions about the *(name of project)*. My telephone number at school is *(number)*. The best time to call me is *(time)*. My e-mail is *(teacher @school.org)*.

Sincerely,
(Name of Teacher)

(Note: If parent permission is needed, it can be solicited below.)

I give my permission for my son/daughter
_____ to participate in the *(name of project)*.
     (print name of son or daughter)

_____ Date _____
          (signature of parent / guardian)

**PARENTAL PERMISSION IS NECESSARY BEFORE
YOUR STUDENT CAN PARTICIPATE IN THE PROJECT.**

PLEASE RETURN TO *(teacher's name)* **BY** *(date)*

TUNING PROTOCOL

1 Choose two groups of four to five students each. These should be groups of students who have worked together on a project or on one aspect of a project.

2 Group A presents, outlining vision, project activities, and outcomes. Group B listens without responding or questioning *(seven minutes)*.

3 Group B asks *clarifying* questions *(four minutes)*.

4 Groups B pauses to reflect on "warm" and "cool" (warm is positive, cool is critical) questions to ask *(two minutes)*.

5 Group B discusses what they have heard *among* themselves, offering warm feedback. Group A takes notes and does not respond *(four minutes)*.

6 Group B discusses what they have heard *among* themselves, offering cool (not cruel) feedback. Group A takes notes and does not respond *(four minutes)*.

7 Group A responds and engages in open conversation with Group B *(four minutes)*.

This method can also be used with three groups. Groups rotate until all three groups have presented and have received feedback. Times can be adjusted according to the needs of the groups, but each step is important.

STUDENT WEEKLY PLANNING SHEET

PROJECT: **STUDENT:** **DATE:**

This week I will work on the following products:

1. Begin By myself

Continue With _____

Complete With _____

2. Begin By myself

Continue With _____

Complete With _____

This week I will carry out the following investigations:

1. Begin By myself

Continue With _____

Complete With _____

2. Begin By myself

Continue With _____

Complete With _____

End of week reflections: what did I learn?

"Student Weekly Planning Sheet" is adapted from The Big Picture Company, The New Urban High School:
A Practitioner's Guide *(Providence, Rhode Island: United States Department of Education, 1998).*

STUDENT PLANNING BRIEF

PROJECT: **STUDENT(S):**   **DATE:**

The overall challenge that defines this project is:

I / we intend to investigate:

I / we need to complete the following activities:

What will I / we do?	How will I / we do it?	Date due

Continued on next page

I / we need the following resources and support:

At the end of the project, I / we will demonstrate learning by:

What?	*How?*	*Who and Where?*

STUDENT LEARNING LOG

PROJECT: STUDENT: DATE:

I had the following goals:

I accomplished the following:

My next steps are:

My most important concerns / problems / questions are:

I learned:

"Student Learning Log" is adapted from materials developed by Autodesk Foundation and Sir Francis Drake High School.

STUDENT INVESTIGATION BRIEF

PROJECT: **STUDENT(S):**   **DATE:**

The question(s) I will investigate:

The data I will collect:	**The method of data collection:**
Who will do . . .	**What?**

How will this investigation take the project to the next step?

STUDENT PRODUCT BRIEF

PROJECT: **STUDENT(S):**   **DATE:**

What product do I / we want to construct?

What research do I / we need to conduct?

What are my / our responsibilities for this product?

Continued on next page

I / we expect to learn the following from working on this product:

I / we will demonstrate what we've learned by:

I / we will complete the product by:

STUDENT PRESENTATION BRIEF

PROJECT: **STUDENT(S):**   **DATE:**

What will the audience learn from my presentation?

(If group presentation) What part am I responsible for?

My plan to make a successful presentation:

Continued on next page

I expect to learn the following from making this presentation:

Specific skills I plan to work on are:

I need the following technology / equipment for my presentation:

I need the following visual for my presentation:

RESEARCH LOG

PROJECT: **STUDENT:**   **DATE:**

Source Record Complete Citation	**Notes** Describe What You Learned

"Research Log" is adapted from The Big Picture Company, The New Urban High School:
A Practitioner's Guide *(Providence, Rhode Island: United States Department of Education, 1998).*

PROJECT MILESTONES

PROJECT:	STUDENT:	DATE:

Milestone	Due Date	Completed
		☐
		☐
		☐
		☐
		☐
		☐
		☐
		☐
		☐
		☐
		☐
		☐
		☐
		☐
		☐
		☐
		☐
		☐

PROGRESS REPORT
FOLLOWING AN INVESTIGATION

PROJECT: **STUDENT:**   **DATE:**

I investigated:

I performed the following steps:

I found out that:

Continued on next page

I learned how to do the following things:

As a result of my investigation, I think we should make the following changes in the project:

GROUPING STRATEGIES

Grouping decisions involve the size of the group, who is in the group, the roles assigned to different group members, and the tasks assigned to the groups themselves.

Different project activities lend themselves to different grouping arrangements. Some activities may best be accomplished by students working by themselves. Other activities may lend themselves to students participating in pairs, in small groups, or as a whole class. Grouping decisions should reflect the nature of the activity and the learning goals envisioned. For example:

Group Size Considerations

SIZE OF GROUP	BEST USES
Individuals (students working alone)	Learning (and teaching) fundamental skills Researching in the library or on the Web
Pairs	Providing one-on-one feedback, editing, peer assessment Providing one-to-one support or training
Small Groups	Working on tasks that have multiple dimensions or steps Sharing perspectives or reaching consensus
Mid-Size Groups	Holding discussions, debates, role-play activities
Whole Class	Presenting orientations, debriefings, progress checks

The location of project activities also influences the size of groups. In many projects, each major activity might have a different location. For example:

Potential Project Sites

LOCATION	USEFUL FOR
In-class	Orientation, coordination, group work, etc.
Home	Generating ideas, revising work, reading, notetaking
Library	Research, reading, using technology
Other classroom	Presenting, getting feedback, gathering data
Community	Gathering data, observing, interviewing, collaborating
With mentor	Modeling, getting advice, getting feedback
With electronic partner	Collaborating, sharing information, getting feedback

GROUP OBSERVATION CHECKLIST

PROJECT: **GROUP MEMBERS:**   **DATE:**

Observe a group for five to ten minutes. Check the boxes that best describe group member participation.	All Members	Most Members	Some Members	Few Members	Not Applicable
When starting a new task, group members					
Agree on an agenda or plan	☐	☐	☐	☐	☐
Begin work promptly	☐	☐	☐	☐	☐
Get out project materials	☐	☐	☐	☐	☐
Figure things out without teacher assistance	☐	☐	☐	☐	☐
Share responsibilities	☐	☐	☐	☐	☐
_____	☐	☐	☐	☐	☐
When conducting research, group members					
Consult primary sources	☐	☐	☐	☐	☐
Take notes	☐	☐	☐	☐	☐
Have relevant conversations	☐	☐	☐	☐	☐
Evaluate the significance of new information	☐	☐	☐	☐	☐
Stay on task	☐	☐	☐	☐	☐
_____	☐	☐	☐	☐	☐
When discussing project work, group members					
Ask clarifying questions	☐	☐	☐	☐	☐
Give each other a chance to speak	☐	☐	☐	☐	☐
Make decisions efficiently	☐	☐	☐	☐	☐
Record decisions and plans	☐	☐	☐	☐	☐
Share essential information	☐	☐	☐	☐	☐
Stay on task	☐	☐	☐	☐	☐
_____	☐	☐	☐	☐	☐

GROUP CONTRIBUTION
SELF-ASSESSMENT

PROJECT: **STUDENT:**   **DATE:**

I have contributed to group progress in the following way:

In this group, it is hard for me to:

I can change this by:

I need to do the following to make our group more effective:

GROUP LEARNING LOG

PROJECT: **GROUP MEMBERS:**   **DATE:**

We had the following goals:

We accomplished:

Our next steps are:

Our most important concerns / problems / questions are:

We learned:

"Group Learning Log" is adapted from materials developed by Autodesk Foundation and Sir Francis Drake High School, San Anselmo, California.

EVALUATION AND REFLECTION
THE FISHBOWL METHOD

1 Arrange students in a large circle.

2 Place a smaller circle of five to seven chairs in the center of the larger circle.

3 Have selected students sit in the inside circle. Keep one chair vacant.

4 Students in the inner circle discuss the outcomes of the project. The audience in the outer circle listens. The vacant chair is for any member of the audience who wants to join the discussion to add a comment or ask a question. Once the comment has been made or the question asked, the participant returns to the audience so that another member of the audience may join the inner circle.

Note that the fishbowl method can also be used for project planning or other tasks that require a group discussion.

END-OF-PROJECT SELF-ASSESSMENT

PROJECT:	STUDENT:	DATE:

I completed the following tasks during the project:

As a result, I learned the following:

About the subject matter

About working in a group

About conducting an investigation

About presenting to an audience

About

Continued on next page

I learned that my strengths are:

I learned I need to work on:

I would make the following changes if I were to do the project again:

PROJECT EXAMPLES

BEGIN WITH THE END IN MIND

CRAFT THE DRIVING QUESTION

PLAN THE ASSESSMENT

MAP THE PROJECT

MANAGE THE PROCESS

Implementing Projects

Contents

PROJECT EXAMPLES

If you want to learn more about specific projects and how PBL works in the classroom, read the examples of PBL on pages 127–147. They include a range of successful projects of varying length from different schools, subjects, and grade levels. Use these exemplars, along with the Project Planning forms, to guide the planning of your own project. Two examples represent projects of shorter duration, carried out in a single classroom. The other two examples describe more complex multidisciplinary projects of longer duration.

The Subtle Media Manipulation Project

11th-Grade English

The Subtle Media Manipulation Project was a six-week project in which students investigated a subculture in American life and the effects of media manipulation on that subculture. The project was tied to the novel *Grendel* by John Gardner, which extended the length of the project. Without the novel, the project would require three weeks to complete.

PROJECT THEME

The project focused on two aspects of American life: the diversity of cultures in the United States and the presence of media forces that shape attitudes and opinions. The project was designed to help students think critically about media, understand the relationship between media and culture, and identify the characteristics of subcultures.

THE DRIVING QUESTION

How do members of a given subculture find meaning in life? What are their values and fears? Given that knowledge, how could government policy-makers, the media, and advertisers successfully manipulate the subculture?

PROJECT OUTCOMES

Students produced a three-part product for the project—including a poem, a proposal, and a log of interviews—designed to deepen students' understanding of media and subcultures, as well as to help them develop writing and reading skills. The outcomes for the project were closely tied to content standards. Key standards were assessed; others were embedded in the project, but not directly assessed.

Your final product will be a proposal to interested parties that will help them know how to manipulate your chosen subculture. It will include the following:

- Title page
- A poem patterned after the Shaper's description of Grendel (the one that gave him his "identity") about the subculture you've chosen
- Proposal (950–1,100 words) that accomplishes the following:
    - Begins with a relevant epigraph from the novel *Grendel*
    - Describes the environment of the subculture
    - Explains how members of that subculture find purpose in their lives as members of the subculture, using observations and quotes from field visits / interviews
    - Proposes a plan, including an ad mock-up, by which media, advertisers, and policy-makers can influence your subculture
- Included after the proposal, three field logs (two interviews, one observation) from visits to the subculture

PROJECT ACTIVITIES

Project activities included helping students look at how media and advertising influence people, and giving students practice in good writing techniques, such as avoiding wordiness and integrating quotes, and structuring essays.

The task for the students was to determine how an advertiser or political consultant could manipulate a subculture based on stereotyping. Students began by reading *Grendel*, along with interviewing members of a subculture of their choice. They then created a poem about the subculture. The purpose of the poem was to identify and reveal the stereotypes, based on knowledge and information from interviews.

The instructions for the poem given to students were: Pattern a poem after the *Beowulf* introduction of Grendel to establish the *idealized identity of your subculture consistent with how its members would like to be identified.* The narrator of the book, Grendel the monster, recounts the experiences that shape his personality as he endeavors to find his purpose in life. One strong force that influences him is a character, the Shaper, who symbolizes the media and demonstrates how the media tells clever lies to manipulate people and, in a sense, to create their identity. This character's influence also extends beyond Grendel; he uses his rhetorical skills to shape the Anglo-Saxon tribe in the book by rewriting their history to make it more favorable to them. Thus, Grendel fits into the exploration of how media exerts influence on people as they seek meaning in their lives—and how advertisers manipulate subcultures by taking advantage of their sense of identity. To assist the students in creating a poem, the teacher provided a copy of the original poem taken from the book, along with an example of how to write the poem based on a *teacher* subculture.

EXAMPLE FOR POEM

The Original Passage

So times were pleasant for the people there until finally one, a fiend out of hell, began to work his evil in the world. Grendel was the name of this grim demon haunting the marshes, marauding around the heath and the desolate fens; he had dwelt for a time in misery among the banished monsters . . .

A Passage Introducing the Teacher Subculture

So times were *ignorant* for the people there until finally one, a *hard-working idealist,* began to work his *knowledge on* the world. Teacher was the name of this *persistent servant, working* all hours, explaining to the little kids and the angry teens; he had dwelt for a time in *frustration* among the *unknowing children*, America's *future*, whom the system had let down and treated as one . . .

Specific examples of how the proposal should be constructed, plus resources, were also provided to students.

GUIDELINES FOR THE PROPOSAL

Introduction, Part One: The Hook
(Intro is one paragraph, 150–200 words, *excluding* epigraph)

You'll use an *epigraph* (sample below) as a hook for this essay. An epigraph is ''a motto or quotation, as at the beginning of a literary composition, *setting forth a theme*'' or ''setting forth your essay's content or spirit.'' The effect of an epigraph is to challenge your reader to determine the relationship between the epigraph and your essay; the epigraph guides their reading and makes them see that you've really considered your point. Once you know where you're going with your essay, look in *Grendel* and choose a quote that *ties in closely with the point your thesis makes* to use as an epigraph.

http://www.bookrags.com/notes/gre/QUO.htm#1 has a list of quotes from *Grendel*. You *might* find what you need there; or, consider which part of the book might contain a quote relevant to your subculture and thesis. The book is full of short remarks that are pithy or witty—you won't have too much trouble finding a good one.

ASSESSMENT AND PERFORMANCE CRITERIA

The assessment rubric for the products was given to students at the beginning of the project to help them focus on the products required in the project and the criteria for performance on each project. Performance criteria were established for the poem and the proposal.

ASSESSMENT CRITERIA

Poem

- Strong "sense of the subculture"
- Alignment with proposal

Proposal

- Introduction: epigraph sets up essay's content and spirit and transitions smoothly; thesis is substantive, contestable, and specific.
- Body: description of environment is vivid; quotes and interviews are used well; analysis is reasonable, balanced, and insightful; thesis is supported.
- Conclusion / influence strategies: thesis is brought back in a purposeful way; possibilities and implications for influence are explained insightfully; ending is satisfying.
- Ad mock-up: knowledge applied is consistent with proposal and interview findings, possesses understanding of effective advertising techniques, and demonstrates neatness and clarity.
- Voice, style, and conventions: voice is consistently aware of audience and purpose; language is concise; there are no or very few minor errors.

On the following page is a list of standards assessed and practiced throughout the project.

STANDARDS ASSESSED

Reading

- Use textual evidence to analyze theme or meaning

Writing

- Write persuasive text that evaluates, interprets, or speculates
- Defend positions with precise, relevant evidence
- Organize ideas in compositions by selecting and applying structures that enhance the central idea or theme
- Write compositions that present complex ideas in a sustained, interesting manner

STANDARDS PRACTICED

Reading

- Apply knowledge of Anglo-Saxon-, Greek-, and Latin-derived roots and affixes to determine the meaning of unknown vocabulary
- Apply knowledge of syntax and literary allusions to understanding new words and comprehending text
- Refine prereading strategies to ensure comprehension
- Analyze historical / cultural influences that have shaped elements of recognized works of literature
- Analyze and evaluate ways authors use imagery, figures of speech, and sound to elicit reader response
- Read and apply multistep directions to perform complex tasks
- Use reading repair strategies, such as summarizing, clarifying ambiguities, and consulting other sources
- Plan for which strategies work best to ensure comprehension of a variety of texts

Writing

- Generate ideas for writing by selecting appropriate prewriting strategies, keeping in mind audience, purpose, and personal style
- Revise writing to improve word choice, organization, and point of view
- Edit for use of standard English
- Apply the rules of usage, grammar, and capitalization with few significant errors
- Use modifiers, parallel structure, and subordination correctly in writing

Listening and Speaking

- Summarize and evaluate communications that inform, persuade, and entertain
- Participate in problem-solving conversations or group discussions by identifying, synthesizing, and evaluating data
- Evaluate possible sources of information for credibility and usefulness

The Hispanic Diabetes Education Project
7th-Grade Science and Technology

In partnership with a local hospital, this middle-school science and technology project engaged students in investigating an important health issue: the increase in diabetes among Hispanic members of the community. The goal of the project was to produce a public service video that would be available to the community through the local cable television station, a brochure, and a booth presentation at a local health fair for Hispanic residents. The project was scheduled to last six weeks.

The project idea originated in discussions and articles highlighting the increasing incidence of diabetes in the Hispanic community. The teacher developed the theme and worked with students to refine the project.

The project began with a visit to the class by a Diabetic Health Instructor from the hospital, which generated interest and concern for the topic among students. During this visit, the class received background information on diabetes and was able to ask clarifying questions about the cause of the disease and its prevention. Through direct instruction, the teacher also provided information on organ systems and the disease process. On previous projects, students had gained expertise in basic video production, interviewing and survey taking, and graphic design.

THE DRIVING QUESTION

How can we educate our community about treatment and prevention measures for diabetes?

STATE SCIENCE STANDARDS—LIFE SCIENCE

Structure and function of living systems: The students know organ systems function because of the contributions of individual organs, tissues, and cells. The failure of any part can affect the entire system.

PROJECT OUTCOMES

The project incorporated state standards for science and writing, and district benchmarks for use of technology. The SCANS skills were used to identify work habits to be learned in the project, along with three habits of mind: persistence, questioning, and creativity. Students were also able to apply Spanish language skills, but these were not formally assessed.

PROJECT PRODUCTS

In addition to completing assignments and taking an exam on the physiology and anatomy of organ systems in the body, students worked in teams to prepare three products. The first product, a video presentation, required the formation of a production company in which a team of students developed the skills of storyboarding, scriptwriting, editing, and graphic production. The production company began by defining roles among team members, such as writer, director, camera operator, editor, and producer. The team conducted biweekly production meetings and posted a visual timeline of their work for other students to see.

A second team conducted research on the prevalence of diabetes and background information on the disease. The team interviewed family members with diabetes and developed a short survey administered in the Hispanic community.

A third team prepared the brochure and booth materials, including booth design and bilingual translations of all products. The three teams periodically met to share progress and information.

PROJECT ASSESSMENT

Rubrics were established for the brochure, video, and booth design products. The teacher and a small team of health professionals from the hospital reviewed and scored all three products.

In addition to teacher observations and class discussions, students' log entries were used as evidence of achievement of skills and habits of mind. Writing skills were practiced and assessed using guidelines developed previously by the language arts teachers.

PROJECT MANAGEMENT

The length and complexity of the project required tight management. Students used interactive notebooks to maintain a log of their progress and reflections of the project. The notebooks were reviewed weekly by the teacher and assessed for content. Each team also had to report progress on a weekly basis, including an update on the storyboard and brochure drafts.

The Up to Par Project

9th- / 10th-Grade Geometry

In this nine-day project, students worked in groups to design a hole for a miniature golf course. Each hole had to allow for a hole-in-one, which was constructed using a compass and the law of reflection.

PROJECT THEME

The challenge of designing a miniature golf course becomes an avenue for exploring geometry concepts and practicing basic math skills, such as angles, reflections, scale drawing, geometric constructions, and proofs. In the context of designing their hole, the students built critical thinking skills, used their creativity, and applied their understanding of math.

THE DRIVING QUESTION

How can we design a miniature golf course and construct the path for a hole-in-one using reflections and angle measurements?

The project took a hands-on approach to learning by having students experiment with a ball bouncing off of a wall, make observations about the rebound of the ball, and formulate a conclusion about the angle at which the ball leaves. Since the scenario of the project had students competing for an internship at a miniature golf course manufacturing company, each group of students had to design a unique and creative hole based on a theme of their choice, which they presented to a panel in a Power Point format.

PROJECT OUTCOMES

The project was designed to meet content standards for geometry. Over the nine days, the project took place in five phases, each of which emphasized a different mathematical skill:

1. Angles
   - Measuring angles with a protractor
   - Classifying types of angles
2. Geometer's Sketchpad
   - Using Geometer's Sketchpad
   - Investigating angles on Geometer's Sketchpad
   - Reflections on Geometer's Sketchpad

3. Scale Drawings
   - Scale factor
   - Enlarging / reducing
4. Reflections
   - Characteristics of reflections
   - Constructing reflections
5. Proofs
   - Two-column proof
   - Paragraph proof

CONTENT STANDARDS ASSESSED

- Students write geometric proofs, including proofs by contradiction.
- Students prove relationships between angles in polygons by using properties of complementary, supplementary, vertical, and exterior angles.
- Students perform basic constructions with a straightedge and compass, such as angle bisectors, perpendicular bisectors, and the line parallel to a given line through a point off the line.
- Students know the effect of rigid motions on figures in the coordinate plane and space, including rotations, translations, and reflections.

PROJECT PRODUCTS AND ASSESSMENT

The project included multiple products that were collected and assessed, including the final presentation using Power Point. Each product was assessed separately, with math assessments based on established criteria. Presentations were assessed through a presentation rubric.

PRODUCTS

- Scale drawing of hole
- Construction of the path for a hole-in-one
- Drawing of hole that labels and identifies all angle types
- Proof showing that the incoming angle is congruent to the outgoing angle
- Power Point that clearly explains the theme and design of the hole

In addition to presentations and drawings, the project required collaboration and written work that enabled teachers and students to meet six overall learning outcomes established for their school:

- **Technology Literacy:** Students used Geometer's Sketchpad software to investigate angles and lines, and used Power Point to create a presentation.
- **Written Communication**: Students submitted a written explanation of their hole design.
- **Oral Communication:** Students presented their hole design and work.
- **Collaboration:** Students worked in small groups to design the golf hole and prepare the presentation.
- **Critical Thinking**: Students used problem solving to construct the path of a hole-in-one and used logic and reasoning to prove that angles were congruent.
- **Math Content**: Students showed understanding of angles and reflections through daily activities, completion of the project, and a test.

The Shutesbury Water Project

6th-Grade Science

The Shutesbury Water Project drew on the experience of teachers at a small, rural elementary school in Shutesbury, Massachusetts.* In Shutesbury, teachers have worked for years to organize the curriculum around PBL. In some years, teachers select a topic to serve as an interdisciplinary theme for instruction across the grades; at the beginning of the year, teachers participate in workshops and field trips so that they all have a common understanding of the theme. For the remainder of the year, kindergarten through 6th-grade students are immersed in the "literary, artistic, mathematical, ecological, political, athletic, scientific, and playful aspects of this broad topic."

PROJECT THEME

Several years ago, teachers at Shutesbury Elementary School chose to study water as their theme. The year was divided into three phases: (1) water as a resource; (2) the physical properties of water; and (3) the biology of bodies of water. Students measured the acidity of local lake and pond water, built and stocked an aquarium with aquatic life, searched for and read literature on water-related topics, and measured water usage and waste by keeping a Water Log.

> **THE DRIVING QUESTION**
>
> How safe is our water?

Having been made aware of the ease with which lakes and ponds become polluted, students posed the question: how safe is our drinking water? Because their region is served by private wells, one for each house in most cases, the question represented a significant challenge for these students. In addressing the question, students were forced to struggle with both scientific and social issues associated with the content of the project, including principles of water pollution, tools and procedures of scientific analysis, the relationship of water quality to public health, and the issues driving community politics.

PROJECT ACTIVITIES

Students and staff decided to test a sample of the private wells in Shutesbury with two concerns in mind: lead and sodium pollution.

*Ron Berger, *Water: A Whole School Expedition* (Shutesbury, Massachusetts: Shutesbury Elementary School, 1996).

School assemblies were held to orient students and answer questions, and students were given instruction in the nature of artesian wells. Students worked with their parents to draw maps of the wells' locations, as well as the slope of the ground, such that a relationship could be drawn between sodium content in well water and proximity to sources of road salt.

Sixth-grade students became experts in techniques of collecting water samples and were also instructed in the proper procedure for taking samples from their family wells. Working in teams, these 6th-graders were taught how to calibrate and use the sophisticated instruments found in the biology laboratory of the local college to test water samples. A separate team of students videotaped the process so other students could be taught these skills. Then, using computer printouts from the laboratory, students created charts and a town map showing the location of every student's home, along with data from the family well. Students were also taught the method of plotting data onto graphs to look for correlations.

Using these charts and their map, students looked for relationships between water depth and sodium content, pH level and sodium content, distance from the road to the well and sodium content, pH level and lead content, and sodium and lead content. Sixth-graders constructed charts to display their findings, which were then used in school assemblies to convey the results to the rest of the school. Proj-

---

CONTENT STANDARDS

- Earth Science: the water cycle.
- Biology: changes in the ecosystem over time.
- Physical Sciences: elements, compounds, and mixtures.
- Technology/Engineering: measurement and the scientific method.

PRODUCTS

The project involved many different kinds of products, from short, individual assignments to formal reports and presentations by groups. Highlights included:

- Town map and charts with data displays.
- Oral presentations to the school and community.
- Written report summarizing findings and answering the Driving Question.

ect activities incorporated a number of technological tools and other resources and took place under a variety of realistic conditions: group tasks, individual work, classroom activities, laboratory tasks, and whole school assemblies. These project activities were essential to address the Driving Question; at the same time, they prompted students to learn central principles associated with the content area.

PROJECT RESULTS

The water project was a great success. Students learned principles of water contamination, the process skills of contaminant testing, the thinking skills of correlational analysis, and the analytic assumptions underlying the pooling of data. They also developed a graphic sense of displaying data and results. In addition, their activities gained them community-wide recognition. Their report on water made it evident that they had been able to successfully interact with university staff, newspaper reporters, and members of the town Board of Health.

The Coming to California Project

11th- / 12th-Grade Humanities

PROJECT THEME

Teachers at Sir Francis Drake High School in San Anselmo, California, wanted to design a ten-week humanities project integrating United States history and American literature in an academy for 11th- and 12th-grade students who were experienced in PBL. After several conversations, they decided to create a multidisciplinary unit on the settlement of California. The teachers knew they wanted to teach students about the history of immigration into the United States; address California's multicultural history; find ways to integrate history, literature, and art; and include a focus on workplace skill standards recently adopted by the district. From a student discussion, themes emerged for the project that reflected questions expressed by students about their history in their community. For example, students observed that resettlement and immigration are normal social processes, and that California itself is a land of immigrants.

PROJECT OUTCOMES

Having considered the big ideas for the project, the teachers next focused on the specific outcomes that they wanted students to achieve. They first examined the content standards for History / Social Science and English / Language Arts. The curriculum standards call for student understanding of the role of diversity in American life and the role of social themes in American literature. From there, the teaching team looked at specific standards for 11th-grade American literature and 11th-grade United States history, including standards relating to immigration patterns and laws. The teachers then developed the project around six content standards.

The teachers were also focused on the competencies and strategies —the *process* skills—that students would learn as they progressed through the activities toward the completion of the project. For specific guidance, the teachers used the list of workplace competencies identified by the Secretary's Commission on Achieving Necessary Skills (SCANS), such as the ability to manage tasks, solve problems, and communicate clearly. From this list, the team identified key skills that would be stressed during the project and—most important—the skills that would be assessed at the end of the project. Finally, the teachers felt that the ability to be more tolerant and understanding of immigrant groups was an important habit of mind or disposition that students could learn from the project. In addition, a ten-week project would be a test of organization and persistence for students.

The outcomes for the project are shown in the following list. All of these outcomes were *simultaneous*—that is, all were an essential part of the project and were assessed.

PROJECT OUTCOMES

Content Standards

- Students read and respond to historically or culturally significant works of literature.
- Students write coherent and focused texts that convey a well-defined perspective and tightly reasoned argument.
- Students deliver polished formal and extemporaneous presentations that combine traditional rhetorical strategies of narration, exposition, persuasion, and description.
- Students analyze the relationship among the rise of industrialization, large-scale rural-to-urban migration, and massive immigration from Southern and Eastern Europe.
- Students analyze the major political, social, economic, technological, and cultural developments of the 1920s.

Skills

- Students will be able to set goals and carry out a project plan.
- Students will be able to deliver an oral presentation in front of a large group.
- Students will be able to generate an interview plan: who, what, where, when, how.
- Students will be able to work effectively in a group and be more disposed to cooperate with peers.

Habits of Mind

- Students will be more tolerant and understanding of immigrant groups.

DRIVING QUESTIONS

The Driving Questions for the project suggested both gaps in teachers' and students' knowledge and activities that would be intriguing for students. Although it is usually easier to focus students' attention on a single question, this topic required multiple Driving Questions.

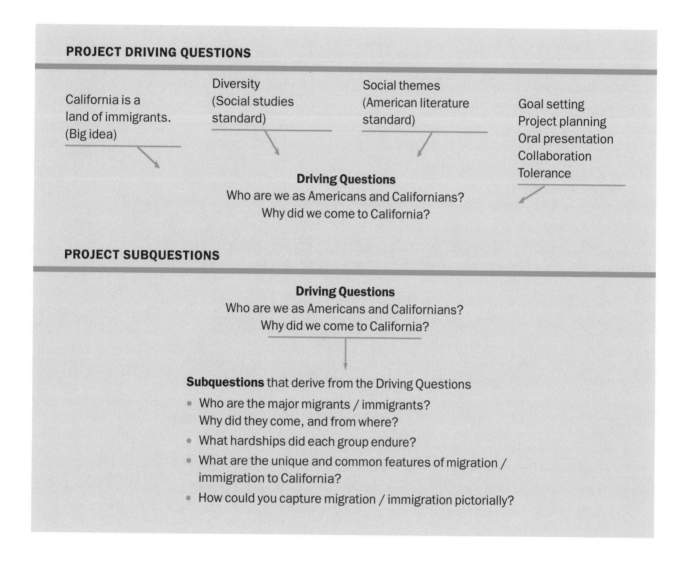

PROJECT DRIVING QUESTIONS

California is a land of immigrants. (Big idea)

Diversity (Social studies standard)

Social themes (American literature standard)

Goal setting
Project planning
Oral presentation
Collaboration
Tolerance

Driving Questions
Who are we as Americans and Californians?
Why did we come to California?

PROJECT SUBQUESTIONS

Driving Questions
Who are we as Americans and Californians?
Why did we come to California?

Subquestions that derive from the Driving Questions

- Who are the major migrants / immigrants?
  Why did they come, and from where?
- What hardships did each group endure?
- What are the unique and common features of migration / immigration to California?
- How could you capture migration / immigration pictorially?

PROJECT ACTIVITIES

To meet the project outcomes, teachers in the Coming to California Project realized that students would need to engage in multiple activities, with different individual and group products submitted for assessment throughout the ten weeks. To accomplish this goal, students were divided into research groups. Each group selected an immigrant / migrant community to investigate, with individual students responsible for one aspect (e.g., cultural contributions, origin, or journey) of that investigation.

Groups were responsible for completing seven interrelated products: (1) an interview summary, results of an interview with a representative from their immigrant / migrant community; (2) a community profile, a description of their selected immigrant / migrant community; (3) a mosaic design, a sketch for a mosaic panel that would capture the story of their community; (4) an essay on *The Grapes of Wrath*; (5) the completed mosaic; (6) a group presentation, an oral report to the class covering the results of their research, interviews, and mosaic design; and (7) individual reports on immigrant / migrant groups (e.g., Chinese Americans and California railroads).

PROJECT PRODUCTS

From the activities, a set of multiple products emerged, including a mosaic with tiles designed by individual groups, group presentations based on research, individual reports, and exams.

COMING TO CALIFORNIA—PRODUCTS

Timeline	Products
Week 1	
Week 2	
Week 3	Interview summary / Quiz
Week 4	Profiles
Week 5	Mosaic design
Week 6	Essay
Week 7	
Week 8	Group presentations / Mosaic
Week 9	Individual reports / Exam
Week 10	

PROJECT ASSESSMENTS

Simultaneous with planning the products from the projects, the teaching team began to look at how to assess what was learned. The assessment of content knowledge, skills, and habits of mind required four types of assessments: performance measures, product assessment, tests, and self-report measures. Rubrics were created to assess products, presentations, and performances.

PROJECT ASSESSMENTS

Assessment Method	Criteria Applied
Tests: Social studies content Literature content (*Grapes of Wrath*)	Knowledge of facts Understanding of concepts
Performance measure: Teacher and student assessment of presentations	Understanding of concepts Critical analysis Collaboration and teamwork
Performance measure: Assessment of mosaic product	Artistic design
Performance measure: Structured observations of group productivity	Effective time management Effective task management
Performance measure: Evaluation of transcript summary and interpretive essay	Completeness Understanding of concepts Integration of concepts Originality of thought
Self-report: Defense of presentation	Effect of project work on understanding of concepts
Self-report: Student questionnaire	Attitudes toward diversity
Self-report: Interview using rubric	Willingness to seek, be sensitive to, use, and benefit from feedback

PROJECT MANAGEMENT

As teachers mapped out the project, they realized that students would need a variety of instructional supports to be able to meet the project outcomes successfully. Skill-building activities were necessary to acquaint students with assessment methods to be used in the project. Discussions about migration and immigration in other parts of the country set the stage for students' research. Other instructional support was introduced during the course of the project, including scaffolding through direct instruction and training in mosaic design and construction using the services of guest artists from the community.

Project management included assembling resources for the project, such as graphics software, computer labs, tape recorders for interviews, videotapes, construction materials, tiles and tools for the mosaic, experts from immigrant / migrant communities, a guest artist with expertise in building mosaics, and school and community representatives who would be the audience for the final presentations.

The Coming to California Project was a large, complex project, lasting several weeks and involving multiple products and assessments. The success of the project was facilitated by a school schedule with 90-minute block periods. Often, two block periods were scheduled back-to-back. This provided substantial amounts of work time for students, a necessity for completing the mosaic. Also, three teachers were involved in overseeing the project.

PROJECT RESOURCES

Product or Activity	Resources
Discussion: Ellis Island	Videotapes of immigration activities
Student research	Computers and Web access
Interviews	Interviewees
Mosaic design and training	Guest artist
Mosaic materials	8' × 10' plywood sheet 10 boxes of tiles Tile cutters Aprons, gloves
Presentations	Panel of experts and community representatives

Three management strategies helped make the project successful. First, teachers closely monitored the pace and direction of project activities using weekly progress reports that included teacher observations, weekly student progress logs, and Friday debriefings. Second, as the teachers mapped out the project, they used five different grouping strategies to ensure greater productivity and accountability. Third, different learning contexts helped students stay enthused during a long project. In addition to working in class and at home, students conducted research in the library and in the community, presented to other classrooms and to the community in an all-school assembly, and worked on the mosaic in a studio near the school.

PROJECT MANAGEMENT

Grouping Strategy	Activities
Individual	Preparing proposals, conducting library research, preparing interview questions, conducting interviews, writing essays, and preparing individual reports
Pairs	Conducting peer critiques
Small groups	Preparing proposals, participating in training, preparing profiles and presentations, and conducting presentations
Small groups with mentors	Training and apprenticeship in mosaic construction
Large groups	Receiving orientations, taking part in team building and discussions, observing presentations, and reflecting on project effectiveness

Context for Project Work	Activities
Classroom	Majority of activities and direct instruction
Homework	Essays, individual reports, and test preparation
Library	Research work for profiles and mosaic design
Community art workshop	Training in mosaic construction and assembly
Community	Interviews
Other classrooms	Mock presentations
Local civic center	Final presentations

Samples of Student Reflection

I really think we understand the big picture about immigrants to California and this country.

I still don't understand the waves of migration. I think we needed a lecture on that.

The Friday debriefings really worked for our group.

We didn't know how to construct a mosaic. We needed more training in art.

The critical analysis rubric was hard to understand. We should redesign it.

The project went on too long.

Samples of Teacher Reflection

Community judges need training in how to use a rubric. They didn't know how to judge the presentations.

Needed a lesson on visual literacy.

The expert groups idea worked really well.

Next time I would build more essays into the project and emphasize peer editing.

PROJECT EVALUATION

Planned as a 10-week project, the Coming to California Project was completed in 12 weeks, with successful presentations and a strong a sense of student accomplishment. A test for content knowledge showed that a majority of students had mastered test and lecture materials on immigration and key historical events, such as the Depression, the New Deal, and the Japanese internments. In presentations, students demonstrated passion, tolerance, and understanding as they related the journey and migration stories of the ethnic group they had chosen to investigate. Many students were motivated to research their own family history in California and relate their findings to immigration topics.

As part of the project planning, the teaching team scheduled one 90-minute period with students to reflect on the project and evaluate the learning that had come from the project. The evaluation was conducted in a community fashion, with students and teachers in a large circle. Students facilitated the debriefing and recorded the discussion.

WHAT DO PBL TEACHERS SAY?

Implementing Projects

BEGIN WITH THE END IN MIND

CRAFT THE DRIVING QUESTION

PLAN THE ASSESSMENT

MAP THE PROJECT

MANAGE THE PROCESS

Contents

WHAT DO PBL TEACHERS SAY?

Comments from experts in the classroom.

T he following are comments gathered from experienced PBL teachers.

BEGIN WITH THE END IN MIND

Get to know your students and their strengths before beginning a project so you can tailor the project to their needs.

- Teachers need to assess students' abilities and interests before beginning a project.
- We start the year in our academy with a mini-project that pairs incoming juniors and returning seniors. We do ten days of team building and getting to know each other. During this time, seniors teach juniors how we work.
- Students have to understand what the need is for the project, and I have to understand what their thinking is before I can get them involved in the project work.
- There will always be students and classes that are quicker or slower than others. Students who move more quickly have more opportunities within projects. You end up having to tailor the curriculum to your classes and sometimes to groups within classes if a group is going very slowly. The same project may look different for different classes or groups because some projects may include additional activities while others omit certain activities.
- If you are teaching students who are less academically able, you have to take this into account when planning the project. The project won't be the same as you might have with an Advanced Placement class. You have to lighten up and find a way for students to use the skills they bring with them. Perhaps they aren't skilled in math but are great writers, or good artists. You can still develop a project so students can express themselves, which will encourage their skill development. You can use the same topics with students of differing ability. But change the final product so that it provides a better match for their skills.

If you or your students are new to PBL, start small.

- Less is more—start small. The project is only part of the picture. You also have to reengineer the learning environment to change the way you work with kids. It's difficult to attack everything at once.

- The advantage of small projects is that you have time to analyze what you are doing, reflect on it, and make adjustments. This should be done in any project, but it's easier with a small project.
- I would advise people to choose one project and do it really well. Don't start out with a lot of projects or a very broad project. Projects get overwhelming and more complicated. You're always trying to rein the project in and get back in control.
- When a teacher is working on his or her first project, it's not necessarily the best thing to involve multiple teachers and make it a collaborative project. The struggle to get the logistics down can undermine the whole project. Once you have experience, collaborate with teachers in other content areas.
- Start by tweaking assignments that you ordinarily give: add some new elements to them. Many teachers can take an assignment that they've given for years and add something to make it more PBL-focused: for example, adding an interview with an adult outside of school when students are doing a research assignment.

To do well in PBL, students have to develop skills not needed in more traditional educational settings. Design incremental projects that give students the opportunity to develop those skills over the course of the year.

- With students who understand PBL or who are mature and ready to participate, you can introduce a project on day one. With others, you have to teach them what PBL is all about. If kids don't know about PBL, I don't introduce a project before October. Before that I have them do mini-units, work on group skills, cooperative learning, and I introduce them to self-monitoring.
- Repeated experiences build on one another. Our students begin projects in the 6th grade. By 8th grade, kids come in knowing how to do projects. I can start at the beginning of the year, and they know the ropes. They know how to work in teams.
- Think of the first project as an icebreaker; don't expect the world. As they work on more projects, kids get more efficient. Things that take two weeks in September will take only one week in April. Student skills improve: getting information, organizing, making decisions.

Plan projects that take place outside the classroom.

- The more you can do outside the context of the school, the more student engagement you have. If you are simply trying to develop skills or learn information that is not connected to current events, then don't do a project. Look through your curriculum for opportunities to take learning outside of your classroom.

Get kids excited about a new project.

- Before starting a project, we get students thinking about it so they'll be ready to plunge in when it's time. Last year, we did a project in April on the physics of music, but we started talking about it in January when the semester began. I suggested a number of questions they might want to pursue, and we discussed how they might form their work groups. The earlier students start thinking about it, the more prepared they are.

- When we start a new school-wide project, we have a kickoff event that gets the students excited about the project and marks it as something different from typical schoolwork.

  BEGIN WITH THE END IN MIND: Part of your new role is not just to teach content, but also to teach kids how to learn content.

  This event has taken different forms. Most recently, we had an assembly and a group of faculty members put on a silly skit. Another time, we had a slide show that demonstrated the diversity of living things. After getting the students interested, we describe the project. We tell them what it's all about and what our expectations are for student work.

Establish a culture that stresses student self-management and self-direction.

- Schools don't necessarily acculturate students to be learners— at least not self-managing learners. We have to undo what's been done to them. In our academy, we have students for two years. We maintain a dialogue with them throughout that period. It can have a lot of starting points: curriculum standards, what kind of a person you want to be, what's required for college, how to study, or working in a high-performance environment.

- Part of your new role is not just to teach content, but also to teach kids how to learn content. The high-achieving kids already know this. They know when they go to the library they have to get more than one book. They know not to choose broad topics like John F. Kennedy because there is too much information available. Your role now is to work with kids who have never tackled a difficult question and teach them the research and study skills necessary to tackle it.

- I had to learn to be patient as students develop adult time management and organization skills. We don't generally teach students how to manage time. In fact, traditional teachers and classrooms set up structures so that students don't need to know how to manage their time—it's managed by the teacher and the bell schedule.

- I had to unlearn the idea that teaching was about my content; I had to learn it was about their thinking. Most of the content students get is dismissed as soon as they graduate (or pass the test). I needed to learn how to help students think through the project work and decide what it is going to look like, and not make all the decisions myself.

- Reengineering the learning environment means moving from the sage on the stage to the guide on the side. It means creating a more collaborative environment with students where projects are a mutual responsibility. You have to rethink your whole relationship with students and become more of a facilitator and coach. Bring the problems to the students to decide rather than solving the problems yourself and bringing the solutions to the students. Make the design of the project itself part of the curriculum. It looks like you are giving up control, but you aren't. You still have ultimate control of things, but you've decided what decisions students are able to make, and you are holding them accountable for making them.

- The transition from being teacher-directed to student-directed takes enormous changes and can be frustrating because there are a lot of new things to learn. I'm trying to become as dependent upon my kids as my kids are on me. At the beginning of the year, kids are very dependent on me. At the end of the year, I want to be dependent on them.

- I had to learn not to give the answers and to ask students more questions—I would want to answer the question for them. I also had to learn not to tell students what to do. You also have to ignore what other teachers think of your chaotic class—you've got kids moving around, going to the library, going to the computer lab.

Create a physical environment that will facilitate project work.

- When we start projects, I create workspaces in my room and make sure I have basic supplies that all students will use.

(As projects progress, students sometimes bring in additional materials from home.) You need files and boxes to keep materials together from each class period. At the end of class, I tell students, "All projects need to be stacked on the center table," and then I move all the projects into specific storage areas for each period. Don't give students the opportunity to touch projects from another period.

CRAFT THE DRIVING QUESTION

- In our projects, we have a single Driving Question. This year it was: "Are people influenced by their society or is society influenced by people?" Students break this down into many smaller questions. They conference with us, and we have to approve their question before they begin. We ask ourselves whether the rephrased question will lead to the depth of understanding we are looking for. We keep sending them back to the drawing board until we think they have a subquestion that will work.

- Teachers must be comfortable with not answering the question. The main purpose for using essential questions is to stimulate students to ponder ideas and issues that are intrinsically complex, and to understand that the search for knowledge is ongoing and does not end when a unit or course is over.

- Every student needs to be able to relate to the Driving Question on some level. The question should elicit multiple perspectives that intrigue and engage a diverse group of students.

- I like to refer back to the Driving Question each day of the project. That way the question becomes a diagnostic for the project: are we making progress toward answering the question?

PLAN THE ASSESSMENT

Design projects that address local, state, and national standards.

- I have the appropriate standards on my desk at all times. Our textbooks predate standards by ten years; they are only a baseline of information; they contain the minimum students are supposed to learn. We intend our projects to teach students more than they would learn from simply reading the text.

- Standards are a part of my world. All teachers have to come to terms with the idea that they have to focus their teaching on frameworks and standards. I set up performance standards at the beginning of the project and then plan assessments. Determine where you want students to be. Then figure out what the indicators are that you can look for and measure.

- A project digs really big holes [into the curriculum]; students go deep, not broad. Make sure students will be going deep into essential standards or important things they need to know.

- First I come up with an idea for a project. Then I think about what could go into it. Then I look at the standards to see what should be covered. (I'm preparing kids for state tests and SATs, so I have to take state standards seriously.) I also look at SCANS and Art Costa's *Habits of Mind*. So I take my idea and ask myself, what do I want students to be able to do at the end of the project besides design a bridge?

PLAN THE ASSESSMENT:

Make sure students will be going deep into essential standards or important things they need to know.

- You need to check your standards to see what you have to cover during the semester. Then you can ask yourself, "What's the best way to cover this? Would a project work?"

- Standards are written as if everything were equal; that's not true. Before we begin a project, we go through the curriculum content for the year and prioritize what kids need to understand. Then we build projects around the content objectives where you want kids to have a deep and abiding understanding, or where a project can meet multiple content objectives.

Include students in planning the project and developing assessment strategies and rubrics.

- Involve students in the planning process to the extent that you can. Teachers can do the planning in broad brush strokes and have students work out the details. Have a written outline of where you are going and a timeline of when you will get there.

- We begin by being clear what curriculum content the project is going to cover. Then we invite students to brainstorm with us. How might we approach this? What skills do we need to learn? This encourages students to "buy in" to the project. Then we look at the different roles needed to complete the project, divide students into teams, and assign roles. We make contractual agreements and get explicit student commitments. Then we ask how we will know if the project is a success. This leads to rubrics that we create with the students. Student involvement changes over the course of the year. On the first project, the teacher does more; as the year goes on, students do more.

- For our government strand, we first brainstormed seven or eight potential project topics (e.g., homelessness, school facilities) with the students. We had a class discussion to set criteria for what we wanted to get out of the project. Then we formed expert groups to look at the topics, and each expert group considered whether a project on this topic could meet the criteria we had agreed to. Each expert group reported, and we narrowed the potential topics down to two. Then we voted as a whole class and selected the topic.

Set clear expectations for students.

- The best way to grade project work is to have a rubric. The rubric should be known in advance by the kids. Students should be involved in developing and refining the rubric. Students should be able to restate a rubric in their own words. Then, when working on a project, they know what they are reaching for and trying to accomplish. They have a standard they can apply to their own work and to the final evaluation.

- The more teachers and students agree on grading criteria before the project begins, and the more transparent the grading criteria is to students—so they really understand what the characteristics of an excellent project are—the better.

- Projects often fail because we (teachers, principals, parents) are satisfied with too little. We don't really push for academic rigor and an authentic learning experience. We need to push ourselves and our kids harder.

Use models to show examples of excellent work.

- Kids won't know what high standards are unless they see them. I try to figure out how to derive models of excellence. You can use the work of previous students. Or, you can use professional work: blueprints done by real architects or poetry written by a local poet. You have to have models, or kids don't know what they are working toward.

- I show them examples of what was done the year before. It boosts the quality of projects—kids want to do better than the kids did last year. I was worried that students would just copy what last year's students did, but seeing previous students' work actually sparked more ideas.

Base project grades on a variety of criteria from a variety of sources.

- We use a variety of assessment methods. We set up rubrics with students at the beginning. We use traditional assessments for written and oral work. We give group grades depending on how their team has done. We give individual grades depending upon students' individual contributions to their groups. We have students grade themselves and assess what they have contributed. We also observe them and rate their workplace skills.

- I use a variety of grading strategies. Everyone gets an individual grade, as well as a group grade. Every student grades every other student in the group. Written and other "academic" work is graded individually along the way using rubrics—it's not considered part of the project grade. The project grade focuses on SCANS skills, self- and group management, organization, and promptness, as well as the final presentation. The grade encourages students to look at the process of how they have worked together and what has been accomplished.

- It's a good idea to give so many grades on a project that the significance of any one grade disappears. Use 15 dimensions to grade a project. Brainstorm these dimensions with students to make sure you've covered everything. Break the project down into many different areas. That way, students don't think of it as an "A" or a "D" project.

- You don't give up testing, essays, or quizzes when you do projects. The important question is, what kind of information will they give you? I uses quizzes, for example, to find out if kids understand things so I can push on. Kids will always need to write essays. Use multiple measures to look for both content and process outcomes. When you give students a description of the project, explain what will be an individual assignment (and graded individually), and what will be a group assignment (with each person in the group receiving the same grade). Also, have students grade themselves and other members of the team. Have the audience at an exhibition grade student work.

- Why should the teacher be the only judge about whether this is a good project? Students tend to be harsher than I do on projects; I blend their judgments and mine for the final evaluation.

- Don't just translate your rubric grade into an A, B, C, etc. Use a wide range of criteria, including affective criteria, to balance things out.

Most teachers weight students' individual contributions more than the team product when calculating grades.

- We favor individual over group grades. Kids want to know how they are doing; they want their own performance rewarded.
- I have 75 percent individual and 25 percent group components to the grade. All students in the same group get the same grade on the final product. All along the way there are individual grades, including tests and quizzes, on important concepts.
- I do not believe in group grades at all. Kids don't like them because somebody can get an A without doing anything while somebody else might get a C after doing all the work.
- I weight group and individual parts of the grade equally. Students need to know that team results matter. If kids know they are going to be evaluated on a project as a whole, they will encourage each other to work.

MAP THE PROJECT

Doing projects doesn't mean abandoning traditional instruction. Choose a mix of instructional strategies based on the outcomes you want students to achieve.

- If you just do projects, kids and parents will complain that the teacher doesn't know anything and is just having students do activities. You need tests, lectures, videos.
- We might spend 40 percent of the time in a traditional classroom environment and 60 percent in project work. Once you set a learning goal, you have to determine what instructional strategy will best meet that goal. Think about what works well in traditional education and what you don't want to lose. Sometimes lectures are appropriate and the most immediate way of communicating information to students.
- It works better for us if we give students direct instruction first to communicate the basic information they need to know to frame and begin the project, and then turn them loose to do the project. This speeds up the project.
- If I can give students needed information quickly (and save time for more important project activities), I'll do it. If a project requires skills and students don't have those skills, I'll remediate to the best of my ability. One time I stopped the project and did a structured reading lesson on how to look for content on the Internet.

- PBL is not a valve you turn on or turn off. It's a continuum. You have to develop baselines of knowledge, build inquiry skills. A project may be running all the time, but at some time during the project, students may be reading a textbook. There are times when PBL is the best way to teach a concept—to show how a system works, for example, or to develop teamwork. There are other times when it doesn't make sense to use PBL— for example, when you are teaching specific algorithms.
- I used to teach all of the content and then introduce the project as an application activity. This didn't work because students didn't retain the content and have it available when they needed it for the project. Now I begin with the project and give students a product they need to create. This creates a need to know.

Projects will take longer than you expect. Leave room at the end of a project to extend project activities.

- When I do a project, I allow enough time at the end in case you have to move back a due date. Don't have an exhibition as a final exam because if you have delays, there's not time for the exhibition.

Planning a project is more complex than planning a traditional lesson: take time, record your plan, use planning templates.

- Initially, it took me several hours of carefully thinking things through to plan a project. I had to decide what I wanted students to produce, what decisions they would make. A school-wide project is even more complex. You need several after-school meetings and need to plan during common preps. Use butcher paper to outline your ideas, record the logistics, and plan the assemblies and field trips. The more people involved, the more you have to write everything down.
- I'm a document person. I write everything down and keep big notebooks. I write down the essential question, then guiding questions, then content standards. I want to write down exactly what I want kids to be able to know and do at the end of the project. This makes it easier to keep on track and make sure students get meaningful things out of the project.
- I use a template to frame my thinking, and I write down my plans. We look at the curriculum, look at the calendar, lay out

what we want students to be able to do and know, consider how the project is going to benefit the community outside my classroom, then plan backwards: how are we going to get from there to here?

- Don't underestimate the value of your students' thinking: don't preplan everything. Be open to student ideas and incorporate them. Let students tumble and learn from their mistakes instead of scaffolding everything in such a way that they are going to be successful. Design learning experiences where they can take more responsibility for the work of learning the content and applying the content outside of school. This produces students who are more resourceful and engaged in their communities.

MAP THE PROJECT:

PBL is not a valve you turn on or turn off. It's a continuum. You have to develop baselines of knowledge, build inquiry skills.

Think carefully about when to schedule a project.

- Projects should not replace end-of-quarter tests or papers; if that happens, then a lot of things are due at the same time and it's counterproductive.
- Almost everybody does projects at the same time. Students complain that they have five projects due in the same week. Teachers should talk to one another and space projects out over the course of the year. This would result in higher quality projects.

Use multiple means to communicate the nature and goals of the project to parents.

- Parents are involved in summer and school-year course and project planning. We have a fall parent meeting (in addition to the regular back-to-school night) to discuss standards for student work and projects. We want the family to understand and buy into the standards we have set for student work. We send material home and stay in close touch with parents. There is a mentor dinner at the end of the third-quarter internship that all parents attend.
- I put the projects up on our school Website. I invite parents to the kickoff meeting where I describe learning goals and expectations. At that time, I tell them what I need from them

and when the culminating event will be. It's important to be up-front and honest that this work will look very different from that of a traditional classroom. This kind of work will require students to make phone calls, write letters, talk with people in the community, meet after school, etc.

- I call each parent before the open house and tell them that I expect them to attend.

- We inform parents using a newsletter, and we put it on the homework hotline and on the Website. We send a letter home with the project calendar, a list of checkpoints that tells when different parts of the project are due, a list of standards by which the project will be graded, and a phone number to call if they have questions. We ask parents to sign the letter and return it so we know they are aware of what will be happening. We send a second letter home with an invitation to parent presentation night near the end of the project.

- At the beginning of the year, I send out a description of the project we're going to do and a parent volunteer slip. Although the students are doing physics projects, you don't have to know about physics to volunteer—parents could tutor kids in PowerPoint, for example. I always have parents view and critique the practice exhibition that takes place about a week before the final exhibition. Parents also show up for open house, and I talk about the projects and display those from previous years.

- We have conversations with parents around first-quarter grades. At that time, we go over what the program is all about. Parents have to understand what students are learning. There is a lot of misunderstanding: "They've completed their learning and now you're doing a project?" You have to show parents evidence that students are learning as they work on the projects.

- When talking to parents about projects, be honest about the tradeoffs you made about the breadth and depth of content covered. All teaching (and projects) require tradeoffs. Kids don't cover as much content if they learn the content in depth. Parents want some kind of a mix between breadth and depth. They don't want their kids' learning to be restricted to a bunch of facts. They want their kids to think and reason.

- Come clean with parents: tell them how you structured the unit to provide both breadth and depth and what you were willing to leave out.

**Use parents and students to find community
and business resources for your project.**

- I use parents as liaisons and get them involved in making community connections and finding out where in the community the project could take place. They have more flexibility outside the classroom. I also encourage older students to make contacts, talk to businesses, and use the phone and e-mail.

- Businesses and other community organizations often do not understand what schools and students are really like. They need to learn about the reality of classrooms before they can provide meaningful help.

- Any outside organization that wants to work with a school needs to come in and spend some time in the school and see the kids. Outside organizations need to understand the range of capabilities we deal with, the nature of discipline, and why schools are structured the way they are. It's nice to theorize, but when they look at a group of 7th graders, they understand whether they are willing to help and what kinds of things they could do. It's frustrating to sit in meetings with people who want to help in the schools but don't understand kids.

- Not everyone makes an effective resource. Different individuals have different things to offer.

- If at all possible, meet with the people in person that you want to help you with your project. Figure out who is an expert, who can come into your classroom and engage students, and who is an expert better suited simply to answering questions—say via e-mail. When experts do come in, prepare students for them.

- Train students to interact with community members. Students need to know how to get funding and support for future projects.

**Don't bring experts in until students
need their expertise to progress.**

- Let the kids get frustrated trying to answer a question that is beyond them, and then bring the expert in. The expert will be treated like a hero.

Block scheduling facilitates project work and teacher collaboration.

- Block scheduling is extremely important, as is having flexible classroom space and computers. We also have a system of permanent passes so kids can go down to the library and move around the campus.

Cross-curricular projects involving multiple teachers require extensive communication and coordination.

- Common planning time, opportunities for structured reflection on project design, teacher research groups investigating student work and projects, and summer planning time are all important project supports.

> MAP THE PROJECT:
>
> I had to learn how to share early with other faculty at the school what we are doing. . . . We were all used to doing things the way we wanted to as teachers, so we had to learn to work with each other.

- I found that a collaborative project worked the best when another teacher and I had the same group of kids in back-to-back periods (a de facto block). We also had common planning periods.
- We hold meetings after school and try to get as many teachers as possible to attend. Everyone has an opportunity to help design and implement the project. Our projects have four main disciplines: Mathematics, Language Arts, Social Studies, and Science. Together, we plan the schedule, the end products, the standards, the checkpoints, and the assessment strategy.
- I had to learn how to share early with other faculty at the school what we are doing. We showed them student work as a way to get into a conversation about teaching and learning. Most teachers don't talk much about teaching and learning. We had to allow dissenters to ask fair questions and had to give them honest answers. We were all used to doing things the way we wanted to as teachers, so we had to learn to work with each other.
- In our academy, we all work in the same physical area and are constantly talking about projects and educational reform. We have formal planning sessions on Wednesday (30 minutes) and Friday (30 minutes). We make adjustments daily.

Projects will take longer—or be over sooner—than you expect.

- The schedule you lay out is never the schedule you follow. It takes experience to know how much flexibility to give students and when to move the project ahead. If projects take forever, kids lose interest and focus. You have to know when to tighten up and maintain deadlines and when to loosen up and say, let's take another week.

- When planning a project, set a certain number of days and build in a 20 percent overrun.

- You've got to keep a flexible project schedule. The weather may not cooperate. Students may complete things faster than you expected. Sometimes kids think they are done and you don't. We've had to give extensions to get expert interviews or because of technology breakdowns. Ideally the project is the outgrowth of other kinds of learning, so you can always reinforce subject matter learning when you can't work on the project.

MANAGE THE PROCESS

As you begin the project, make sure all students are on the right track.

- The first day of the project is a warm-up. I have kids brainstorm questions and complete a research plan. I don't send them to the library until I'm sure they know why they are going there. Before they go anywhere outside the classroom, I have their time organized for them: "Here's your research topic for today. I'm going to check your notes at the end of the period."

- I have a private meeting with each group to get them started while the rest of the class is involved with a reading assignment. I discuss each group's research questions with them. Students often don't know what a good research question is. You have to tell them if they have written a question that is really hard to research. I say, "Try it if you want, but here are my suggestions."

- At the beginning of a project, we require a product to be completed out of each work session. If it's a research period of one and one-half hours, we'll require them to make an oral group report about what they've learned. Or, we ask them to write an action plan. After they get used to our expectations, we will let them go for a couple of periods before asking for a report.

- Projects often fall apart because teachers don't pay enough attention to scaffolding students. A great deal of thought needs to be given to how to support students through coaching and mentoring. Students need to have milestones and benchmarks, perhaps even templates.

Tailor your grouping strategies to the needs of the project.

- We use a variety of grouping strategies in the course of the year; sometimes the teacher chooses group members, sometimes students choose. We generally use heterogeneous grouping. Putting the higher academic kids with the lower kids brings the lower kids up yet doesn't hurt the upper kids. It also makes the school more pleasant because kids make new friends. We let kids pick groups initially, but we're constantly reforming teams. Kids change in the course of a year; people change friends.

- One type of grouping strategy—say, kids who are friends and want to work with each other—works well on a task that requires a great deal of time out of school. A different type of group is necessary if the task is complex and requires a diverse set of skills—say the researching of a complex topic and the creation of multimedia and written reports. Think about the skills necessary to accomplish the task at hand when forming a group.

- You first have to think about the purpose of forming groups. We always controlled group characteristics. We had both juniors and seniors. We wanted seniors (who were experienced with projects) mixed in with juniors so they could teach them the ropes. Other teachers have each student pick another student to form a pair, and the teachers put different pairs together into four-person groups. This way, both teachers and kids have control over how the groups are formed. My general experience is that three- or four-person groups work best.

- Think about why you are grouping kids before you do it. Make it appear random, but be highly manipulative in the background: choose "random" techniques that will split problem kids apart. (By making the grouping appear "random," you take the heat off yourself.) Select strengths within groups, but don't let kids exercise only their strengths. Have kids reflect upon what they are strong and weak in: target their weaknesses, don't just celebrate their strengths.

- We formed students into expert teams who investigated different areas and thus became experts. Then we formed new teams that had one member from each of the expert teams. That way, each new team had an expert in each of the areas originally investigated.

- Teachers know students better than anyone else, and they are in the best position to decide how to group students based on the project goals. You can group all the assertive students in one group, and then break the remaining students down by how much support they are going to need from you. You can group by gender. You can group by ability—making a heterogeneous group with a high, medium, and low student in each group. If all of the students are going to do all of the work, then there's no reason to group students except to provide a way to share ideas.

- When it is time to work in groups on a project, I think about why I'm grouping and what the group needs to accomplish. My experience is that if you allow students to choose their own groups, there will be some strong, mature groups and some wacky, immature groups. The strong groups wind up running the show. I don't want this to happen.

- I want leadership to rotate and be shared. When it was time to do water testing in a nearby stream, I put together field teams that had kids who were leaders, kids who needed leadership, conceptually strong students, and weak students. The kids complained, but the project itself—doing water testing—was so compelling that they didn't complain too much. Another part of the project required students working together over several weeks, putting data in spreadsheets, thinking about things, sharing ideas. I decided it would be OK for them to be with their friends, but I didn't want to have them simply choose their friends because some kids wouldn't get chosen. So I had them apply to work with one another. Then I looked at their choices and made up the groups. This way, I was able to place the unpopular or behaviorally challenged kids in appropriate groups.

- Being in a socioeconomically challenged situation where transportation is a problem, students work outside of school, and they have to mesh their schedules to find time to work together. I find there are fewer difficulties when they form groups that enable people to get together. Even though I allow students to choose their partners, I think it's important for the students in the group to have a variety of skills. I have them do an inventory during their first group meeting of their strengths and weaknesses. Then I tell them what they are going to have to be able to do to complete the project successfully, then ask the groups if they have the mix of abilities they need. Sometimes groups reform so that they will have skills they were lacking.

Plan how to accommodate the needs of diverse students.

- I plan a group project so there's time for remediation with kids who just don't get it.
- We can cover a semester's material through lecture and discussion in less than 18 weeks, but if you allow time for kids to do

their project, as well as to internalize the material, it takes the entire semester. While we're working, I give special attention to some kids and simply direct others to resources. I also have kids develop a portfolio so they can refer to it when they need something we've already covered.

- Students can get help from other group members, they can go to the teacher and say, I need help, or they can ask for time to go to the library.

- You have to start students where they are and accept this. You then measure how much growth they've made. An F student can learn more than an A student. Try to find areas where students can shine.

- Try to make it possible some of the time for students to either work with their friends or work on a topic they are particularly interested in.

- We typically form groups according to whom students want to work with, although we have to do a bit of shuffling sometimes. Not everybody gets his or her first choice. Students submit to us their first and second choices of partners, and then we balance out the groups to get the strengths needed.

- We put out a list of topics and ask kids to rank them. We form groups so that every student gets to work on something they want, but they don't necessarily get to work with whom they want.

If individual group members don't carry their own weight, fire them!

- I sometimes allow groups to fire individual members. That's like a business—the project takes precedence over everything. Once they are off the team, they have to do more traditional learning activities. If a student is not working in a group, take them out of the group. This can help the current project you're working on, but the same problem may arise with the next project.

If individual group members aren't working, talk with them (and their parents) about their behavior.

- When a student complains that another student in the group is not working, I bring the entire group in and say, "I've noticed that you are all not doing the same thing. Let's renegotiate the timeline. (Renegotiate means 'tighten up.') On this date (in the near future) you are going to come in at lunch, and I'm going to give you a grade on what you've completed."

- When necessary, I call parents at home to let them know what's happening with the project (and, sometimes, tell them that their child has missed some checkpoints). I remind the parent that it's the child's responsibility to stay on track with the project and ask for suggestions about what the parent and I can do to help the child manage himself or herself better. For some kids, even this doesn't work. I believe middle school is a time for kids to make choices, and if they choose to fail, I'll give them a poor grade.

- I've never been in a group where everybody carried his or her own weight. This is not just a student problem. Students should know that they can come to you for intervention if they can't work it out among themselves as group members. This is something that should be dealt with early by the group and by the teacher if necessary.

- It's inevitable that not everyone in the group will carry his or her own weight. I deal with it by having individual and group reflection and critiques about process and product. I don't want to find out two months later that someone isn't working. I try to use peer pressure: groups have to get up and talk about where they are and what they're finding out. If someone isn't pulling his or her own weight, then it emerges. There are lots of checkpoints, so I can make sure people are on track.

MANAGE THE PROCESS:

I've never been in a group where everybody carried his or her own weight. This is not just a student problem. Students should know that they can come to you for intervention if they can't work it out among themselves.

- You can't just tell a kid, "You have to start working." They'll feign work while you're there and then stop. If you ask them why they aren't working, they may tell you. They may not. It's a fine art of working with and motivating an individual. You just have to use all the tools you can. You can get everybody to sit down and ask the group, "How are we going to get you guys going again? I've been watching you for two periods and I haven't seen anything happening. What are we going to do about this?" Once you identify the issues, you can work with the student using conversation and encouragement. No kids want to be failures unless they are having extreme emotional problems. If you can't get a group restarted, then ask them, "Is there an alternative, individual way of working on this project that will show me you've learned that material?" Students often don't want to work by themselves because it's not as much fun as working in a group.

Keep track of each group's progress.

- I manage groups by running around madly—it's like having ten pots on the stove and trying to stir each one. Students are working on computers at different locations in the school. I move around, see what they are doing, put out fires. There's no magic except for knowing which groups need more guidance and which are more independent.

- I manage groups by setting clear benchmarks and due dates, and holding "touch-ins" (short conferences) with groups on a regular basis. Some teachers set aside one day a week for a student-run discussion of group progress, problems, and opportunities.

- One approach is to have groups complete a planning form together that asks what they are intending to do over a specific time period, what resources they will need, how they will evaluate their progress, etc., and then the teacher conferences with each group using this planning form. I found 3 × 5 cards are handy to record observations of group progress and problems, as are clipboard checklists. Individual students and groups of students can be held accountable for self-reflection and management or redirection of their activities. The goal of good management is to work smarter rather than harder. There isn't a cookbook here. You have to figure out what will work in your class with your students. If kids are not at some reasonable level of self-management, you won't be able to conference with individual groups because that means turning your back on other groups. You probably won't get it right the first time, so you should be prepared to readjust your group management strategy. It's very powerful when students see that adults also have to adjust their strategies when they don't work out.

- I keep a folder for each group that tells what's going on. It tells what the group did each day and what the group will do tomorrow. Groups also have folders recording what they have to do, what they have to accomplish. When I meet with groups, we go over the work in their folders, check off what they accomplished against what they said they were going to do, and assess the quality of the work they completed.

Make sure groups keep track of their own progress.

- Most of my group meetings are outside of class. I require my groups to keep a log that tells who was present, what they accomplished, and the agenda for the next meeting. I check these when I conference with the group.

Keep public records of group progress.

- I keep my records public so students have ownership of them. I use checklists that describe each component in a project. (A student will have to complete eight to ten components to complete the project.) When they complete each component satisfactorily, it is checked off. I put a student in charge of the progress chart. I'll have a class meeting and ask the student in charge of the progress chart to give an update of where everyone is. By making it public, there's no getting away from the accountability, and kids push each other. It's not just me nagging them.

- On a typical day, we'll spend five minutes setting the period's objectives, then two hours of work, and five to ten minutes at the end of the period where we check off what the group has accomplished. We expect groups to be able to say, this is what I found out and whether or not they met the objectives they set.

- I like to have graphic displays that show the whole class every group's progress. Anyone can walk over to see where groups are and what they have accomplished. It's also a way to show groups that they are on common ground (or have completed something important) and thus encourage group collaboration and resource sharing.

The Internet is only one information resource.
Students often need help using it efficiently.

- The Internet is a prime resource, but the school library or media center often has better information than the Internet. The librarian or media teacher has to be a project partner, brought in from the beginning and told what their role will be and how they can help.

- Students have to learn to find information on the Internet efficiently. For our projects, we don't just turn students loose and say, go look up something. First, we preview Websites that might be helpful and then give them a list of sites to start with. Otherwise, they spend a lot of time on false starts.

- Often kids look at Websites, but they don't have the prerequisite knowledge and vocabulary to understand what they are seeing. You have to coach them. Kids aren't aware that the quality of information available on the Internet varies tremendously.

- You have to work with students so that they evaluate the quality of information available and consider multiple sources to see if they are in agreement. In general, kids are too prone to use the Internet and ignore print resources.

Technology can be a powerful tool.
It can also crash and leave you stranded.

MANAGE THE PROCESS:

It's important not to let the bells and
whistles be the central focus of the
project. Content slips away if there is
too much emphasis on technology.

- It's helpful to have technology experts on call; glitches can really slow you down. You have to try out the technology yourself before asking students to use it. You can easily waste a whole period when the technology doesn't work as you had expected it to.

- You'd better have somebody who can trouble-shoot the technology. If the lab or the computer goes down, and you can't troubleshoot the problem yourself, you'll lose student work. Technology is dicey stuff. If you don't really know it, you'd better have a partner who does. It doesn't matter how fabulous technology can be if it results in utter frustration and no learning.

Think about how technology will make your project
more effective. Don't use technology blindly.

- Let the meat of the project decide how technology is to be utilized. Don't think that in order to make a project successful one needs to use technology; community experience is more important than technology.

- It's important not to let the bells and whistles be the central focus of the project. Content slips away if there is too much emphasis on technology. The important question to ask is, what can be accomplished using a technological (or any other) tool? For example, we had kids use an authoring program to create a computer-based interactive presentation focusing on a 20th-century American poet. Viewers could select academic background, the biography of the poet, students' analysis of his or her poems, a video about the poet, and then enter their own comments about the presentation. This was an example where technology let us create a product that could not be created without it.

- If you are going to include technology, you have to have lab time planned for kids to master it. Give limited, specific amounts of time in the lab. Have an assignment for each lab period—don't just turn students loose. Make them turn in a design brief before they can use the computer.

- Use technology only when it is appropriate. Make sure the computer can do it better. Make sure the information sources

are tailored to the information needed. The Web may not
be as good as the library for information on a 16th-century
explorer.

Don't be afraid to make mistakes.

- There is no "cookie-cutter" way to do projects. Don't be afraid
  to make mistakes. Initially I thought I was doing a disservice to
  students if I had something that didn't work. Now I realize it's
  better to make a mistake and discuss with students what needs
  to be changed to make it work. This has also improved my
  relationship with students—it's more collegial now.

Don't be afraid of making midproject corrections.

- When it is apparent that students are missing something they
  need to know for the project, we have a whole class meeting
  and say, "OK, we've discovered that you are missing essential
  information, so let's take a day and do direct instruction on
  what you are missing." It's important to be transparent to the
  students: we missed it; let's do it now.
- If key things are not understood, stop the ship and say, "Time for
  a midcourse correction." You might want to give a lecture; you
  might want to have a class discussion about an important book.
  If you have an ongoing assessment model in place so you are
  periodically checking in with students and they are checking in
  with themselves, you will know whether the project is going
  according to plan. If students aren't getting something, address it.
- I sometimes make major changes in my projects when they are
  under way. Students may realize that it isn't feasible to do what
  they wanted to do. Or, they realize that they want their project
  to be more complex and inclusive than they had originally
  planned. In these cases, we rework the timeline and give groups
  extensions so they can redo their projects.
- When a problem arises, I have a class meeting to debrief the
  incident and reassess the project. This opens up the student /
  teacher relationship and enables you to start with a new
  beginning. Sometimes it's hard to face the fact that your project
  isn't working as you had planned, but you have to bite the
  bullet, recognize a failure, and turn the failure into success.
  Focus on why the failure occurred, and help students overcome whatever was blocking them (e.g., time management,
  organization, diligence, writing skills, etc.).

- Once a project is under way, you may realize that some groups are not going to complete the project as you had expected. We then negotiate what is critical to accomplish and what would be nice to accomplish. Sometimes projects fall apart because of factors outside your control. E-mail partners stop responding. Technology goes down. It's important for groups to explain to the community audience at the culminating event why they didn't get to the goals they had set. Typically, midcourse corrections are more minor than major because you are having ongoing conferences with individuals and groups, and these allow you to address and resolve problems when they are still small.

Debrief the project with your class and note ideas for improvement.

- I typically ask two questions when the project is complete: 1) what do you see of lasting value as a result of this project for yourself as a learner? and 2) what do you see of lasting value as a result of this project for the community? I also have a comment box and solicit suggestions from audiences, students, or observers about how we could do things better.
- I show students good models of reflection that other kids have done. Once they know what quality reflection looks like, I ask them to reflect on their own work. The last part of the reflection asks them to select five projects done by other students in the class and describe what it was about those projects that impressed them. I emphasize the fact that if they are always choosing projects done by their friends, they're not being honest. Kids don't always want to write about what they've done, but they love to write about other projects they liked and tell why.
- Conversation and oral reflection is essential. Often you don't know what you are thinking until you say it out loud. You need to think about and answer the question, "Why didn't this work?"
- At the end of a project, we spend one-half or more of a period talking about what students have done well. This is really important after a technology project where kids work very hard for five days, but their animation is of poor quality. From looking at it, you can't tell whether they worked hard or threw it together. Reflection is also an important place for kids to say

what didn't go right, for them to tell you things they want you to know when they are being graded, and to find out how they would grade themselves and their partners and why. It's also a good time for students to tell you their complaints.

- Students always ask: is this going to be on the test? or how many points is it worth? Postproject reflection is a way to move the focus of discussion to "Here's an end product. Are you proud of it? Did it do what you set out to do? How could it be made better? How could project activities have supported your work better?" Class reflection also provides feedback for the teacher. Maybe we should have talked about something earlier instead of waiting until the last week. Kids are going to do projects their whole life. They need a chance to think about what they've done and how they can do better.

- I give kids "post-its" and have a "post-it session." Kids write comments, walk around, and put them on other students' projects. We also debrief the project as a whole class, both the process of the project, as well as the results. Students also write about the project itself, what worked, what they would do differently about getting the information they need. I have a project critique form that gives space for students to talk about how the different parts of the project worked.

- I also make notes constantly in my own binders regarding what I wouldn't use next year or where I need additional resources. I keep the student feedback sheets in a notebook. I review these during the summer when I'm planning for next year's work.

- Teachers don't put enough time and energy into really questioning what they've done, what the learning was, what kids thought was important. You have to take time to process what you've done.

Reflecting on the Driving Question

- Reviewing the Driving Question at the conclusion of a project is a great way to enhance learning and retention. Plus, it makes students think about the big issues in life and how challenging they can be to solve.

ACKNOWLEDGMENTS

In addition to John Thomas, PhD, we wish to thank the following individuals for contributing teacher comments:

Clarence Bakken
Ron Berger
Bill Bigelow
Will Fowler
Stephan Knobloch
Kate McDougall

Dave Moore
Adria Steinberg
Michelle Swanson
Leslie Texas
Melissa Wrinkle

PROJECT PLANNING FORM

BEGIN WITH THE END IN MIND

CRAFT THE DRIVING QUESTION

PLAN THE ASSESSMENT

MAP THE PROJECT

MANAGE THE PROCESS

Implementing Projects

Contents

PROJECT PLANNING FORM

The Project Planning Form that follows can be used to plan out your project. This form is also available from the BIE Website, www.bie.org.

PROJECT PLANNING FORM

Project title: _____

Teacher(s): _____

School: _____

Grade level(s): _____

Subjects: _____

Begin with the End in Mind

Summarize the theme or "big ideas" for this project.

Identify the content standards that students will learn in this project (two to three per subject).

Identify key skills students will learn in this project.
List only those skills you plan to assess (two to four per project).

Identify the habits of mind that students will practice in this project (one to two per project).

Identify district outcomes or school-wide outcomes to be included in this project.

● *Does the project meet the criteria for standards-focused PBL?*

Craft the Driving Question

State the essential question or problem statement for the project. The statement should encompass all project content and outcomes, and provide a central focus for student inquiry.

● Have you posed an authentic problem or significant question that engages students and requires core subject knowledge to solve or answer?

Plan the Assessment

Step 1: Define the products and artifacts for the project:

Early in the Project:

During the Project:

End of the Project:

Plan the Assessment

Step 2: State the criteria for exemplary performance for each product:

Product:

Criteria:

Product:

Criteria:

Product:

Criteria:

Product:

Criteria:

● *Do the products and criteria align with the standards and outcomes for the project?*

Map the Project

Look at one major product for the project and analyze the tasks necessary to produce a high-quality product. What do students need to know and be able to do to complete the tasks successfully? How and when will they learn the necessary knowledge and skills?

Product:

KNOWLEDGE AND SKILLS NEEDED	ALREADY HAVE LEARNED	TAUGHT BEFORE THE PROJECT	TAUGHT DURING THE PROJECT
		(Check appropriate box)	
1.			
2.			
3.			
4.			
5.			
6.			
7.			
8.			
9.			
10.			
11.			

What project tools will you use?

- ☐ Know / need to know lists
- ☐ Daily goal sheets
- ☐ Journals
- ☐ Briefs
- ☐ Task lists
- ☐ Problem logs

- ☐ _____
- ☐ _____
- ☐ _____
- ☐ _____
- ☐ _____
- ☐ _____

● *Do the products and tasks give all students the opportunity to demonstrate what they have learned?*

Map the Project

Draw the storyboard for this project, with activities, resources, timelines, and milestones.

Use the Tuning Protocol with other teachers or a group of students to refine the project design or guide you further in your planning. What other thoughts do you now have on the project?

● *What challenges or problems might arise in this project?*

Manage the Process

List preparations necessary to address needs for differentiated instruction for ESL students, special-needs students, or students with diverse learning styles.

How will you and your students reflect on and evaluate the project?

- ☐ Class discussion
- ☐ Fishbowl
- ☐ Student-facilitated formal debrief
- ☐ Teacher-led formal debrief
- ☐ Student-facilitated formal debrief
- ☐ Individual evaluations
- ☐ Group evaluations
- ☐ Other: _____
- ☐ _____

● *What do you expect to learn from this project?*